ALL-IN-ONE
Implementing and Administering Cisco Solutions
CCNA Exam 200-301 Cert Guide

1st Edition

Copyright © 2021 CCIEin8Weeks
All rights reserved.
ISBN: 9798674521808

Our Cisco Next-Level Certifications Catalog

Our Cisco DevNet Certifications Catalog

Contents at a Glance

Chapter 1 Network Fundamentals
Chapter 2 Network Access
Chapter 3 IP Connectivity
Chapter 4 IP Services
Chapter 5 Security Fundamentals
Chapter 6 Automation and Programmability

Table of Contents

About the Author 12
Preface 13
What this Study Guide contains 14
How to use this Study Guide 15
What's available on the CCIEin8Weeks website 15
CHAPTER 1 NETWORK FUNDAMENTALS 17
    Explain the role and function of network components 19
        Routers 19
        Process and CEF Switching 20
        Software-based CEF 21
        Hardware-based CEF 21
        FIB vs. RIB 22
        L2 and L3 switches 23
        Next-generation firewalls and IPS 23
        Access points 26
        Cisco WLAN infrastructure consists of either autonomous (standalone) or lightweight APs (LAPs) that are connected to the network via WLAN controllers. The autonomous APs are also known as Fat APs. 26
        Controllers (Cisco DNA Center and WLC) 26
        Endpoints 27
        Servers 27
    Describe characteristics of network topology architectures 27
        2-tier 29
        3-tier 31
        Spine-leaf 33
        WAN 33
        Small office/home office (SOHO) 34
        On-premises and cloud 34
    Compare physical interface and cabling types 34
    Identify interface and cable issues (collisions, errors, mismatch duplex, and/or speed) 38
    Compare TCP to UDP 39
    Configure and verify IPv4 addressing and subnetting 40
    Describe the need for private IPv4 addressing 41
    Configure and verify IPv6 addressing and prefix 43
    Compare IPv6 address types 44
        Global unicast 44
        Unique local 44
        Link local 44
        Anycast 45
        Multicast 45

    Modified EUI 64 45
  Verify IP parameters for Client OS (Windows, Mac OS, Linux)........................45
  Describe wireless principles 47
    Nonoverlapping Wi-Fi channels...47
    SSID 48
    RF 49
    Encryption...50
  Explain virtualization fundamentals (virtual machines) 50
    Hypervisor Type 1 and Type 2 52
    Virtual Machine 53
    Containers 55
    Docker Containers 56
  Describe switching concepts 59
    MAC learning and aging..59
    Frame switching...60
    Frame flooding...61
    MAC address table..61
  Chapter Summary..64

CHAPTER 2 NETWORK ACCESS 67
  Configure and verify VLANs (normal range) spanning multiple switches 69
    Access ports (data and voice)...69
    Default and Native VLANs..69
    Connectivity 69
  Configure and verify interswitch connectivity...70
    Trunk ports 70
    802.1Q 71
    Native VLAN 71
  Configure and verify Layer 2 discovery protocols (Cisco Discovery Protocol and LLDP) 71
  Configure and verify (Layer 2/Layer 3) EtherChannel (LACP)........................73
  Describe the need for and basic operations of Rapid PVST+ Spanning Tree.....................74
    Protocol and identify basic operations 74
    Root port, root bridge (primary/secondary), and other port names.....................75
    Port states (forwarding/blocking)...75
    PortFast benefits 76
    Further Reading 76
  Compare Cisco Wireless Architectures and AP modes 76
    Centralized (Local-Mode) Model 77
    Distributed Model...79
    Controller-less Model 80
    Controller-based Model 80
    Cloud-based Model..80
    Remote Branch Model 81
    SD-Access Wireless Model...83
    Location services in a WLAN design...84

Further Reading 84
Describe physical infrastructure connections of WLAN components (AP, WLC, access/trunk ports, and LAG) 84
Describe AP and WLC management access connections (Telnet, SSH, HTTP, HTTPS, console, and TACACS+/RADIUS) 87
Configure the components of a wireless LAN access for client connectivity using GUI only such as WLAN creation, security settings, QoS profiles, and advanced WLAN settings 89
Further Reading 92
Chapter Summary 93

CHAPTER 3 IP CONNECTIVITY 95
Interpret the components of routing table 97
Routing protocol code 97
Prefix 98
Network mask 98
Next hop 98
Administrative distance 98
Metric 98
Gateway of last resort 99
Determine how a router makes a forwarding decision by default 99
Longest match 99
Administrative distance 99
Routing protocol metric 100
Configure and verify IPv4 and IPv6 static routing 100
Default route 101
Network route 101
Host route 101
Floating static 101
Configure and verify single area OSPFv2 101
Multiple Areas 103
Route Summarization 105
Inter-area Route Summarization 105
External Route Summarization 106
Further Reading 107
Route Filtering 108
Further Reading 111
Describe the purpose of first hop redundancy protocol 111
FHRP Best Practices 113
HSRP Configuration 114
HSRP Verification 114
VRRP Configuration 116
VRRP Verification 117
Chapter Summary 118

CHAPTER 4 IP SERVICES 120
Configure and verify inside source NAT using static and pools 121

  Static NAT 122
  Dynamic NAT 122
  Static PAT 123
  PAT (NAT Overload) 124
 Configure and verify NTP operating in a client and server mode 124
 Explain the role of DHCP and DNS within the network 125
 Explain the function of SNMP in network operations 127
 Describe the use of syslog features including facilities and levels 128
 Configure and verify DHCP client and relay 129
 Explain the forwarding per-hop behavior (PHB) for QoS such as 130
 classification, marking, queuing, congestion, policing, shaping 130
 Configure network devices for remote access using SSH 131
 Describe the capabilities and function of TFTP/FTP in the network 132
 Chapter Summary 134

CHAPTER 5 SECURITY FUNDAMENTALS **136**
 Define key security concepts (threats, vulnerabilities, exploits, and mitigation techniques)
 137
  Viruses 138
  Trojans 138
  DoS/DDoS Attacks 139
  Phishing 142
  Rootkits 143
  Man-in-the-Middle (MiTM) Attacks 143
  SQL Injection (SQLI) 143
  Cross-site Scripting (XSS) 144
  Malware 145
  Data Breaches 146
  Insecure APIs 146
  Compromised Credentials 147
 Describe security program elements (user awareness, training, and physical access control) 147
 Configure device access control using local passwords 148
  Configuring login authentication and authorization using a local database on Cisco IOS XE 148
  Configuring login authentication and authorization using a remote RADIUS server on Cisco IOS XE 149
 Describe security password policies elements, such as management, complexity, and password alternatives (multifactor authentication, certificates, and biometrics) 149
 Describe remote access and site-to-site VPNs 150
  Verifying GRE/IPSec Configuration 153
 Configure and verify access control lists 154
  Further Reading 155
 Configure Layer 2 security features (DHCP snooping, dynamic ARP inspection, and port security) 155

      Dynamic ARP Inspection (DAI) 155
      Port Security 156
  Differentiate authentication, authorization, and accounting concepts 157
  Describe wireless security protocols (WPA, WPA2, and WPA3) 157
  Configure WLAN using WPA2 PSK using the GUI 158
  Chapter Summary 160

CHAPTER 6 AUTOMATION AND PROGRAMMABILITY 162
  Explain how automation impacts network management 163
  Compare traditional networks with controller-based networking 163
  Describe controller-based and software defined architectures (overlay, underlay, and fabric) 164
      Further Reading 168
  Separation of control plane and data plane 168
  Compare traditional campus device management with Cisco DNA Center enabled device management 171
      Further Reading 178
  Describe characteristics of REST-based APIs (CRUD, HTTP verbs, and data encoding) 178
      Further Reading 181
  Recognize the capabilities of configuration management mechanisms Puppet, Chef, and Ansible 182
  Interpret JSON, XML and YAML encoded data 188
      XML Example 189
      XML Prologue 190
      XML Comments 190
      XML Body 190
      XML Attributes 191
      XML Namespaces 191
      JSON Example 191
      JSON Data Types 192
      JSON Objects 192
      JSON Maps and Lists 192
      YAML Example 193
      YAML File Structure 193
      YAML Data Types 193
      YAML Indentation and File Structure 193
      YAML Maps and Lists 193
      YAML Comments 194
      XML Parsing in Python 195
      Using the ElementTree APIs to parse XML 196
      Using Minidom Module to parse XML 198
      JSON Parsing in Python 199
      YAML Parsing in Python 201
      Further Reading 203
  Chapter Summary 204

About the Author

Muhammad Afaq Khan started his professional career at Cisco TAC San Jose and passed his first CCIE in 2002 (#9070). He held multiple technical and management positions at Cisco San Jose HQ over his 11 years of tenure at the company before moving into cloud software and data center infrastructure IT industries.

He has worked at startups as well as Fortune 100 companies in senior leadership positions over his career. He is also a published author (Cisco Press, 2009) and holds multiple patents in the areas of networking, security, and virtualization. Currently, he is a founder at Full Stack Networker and a vocal advocate for network automation technologies and NetDevOps. He is a Cisco Certified DevNet Associate[1] and was among the first 500 people #DevNet500 worldwide to pass the exam.

 Cisco Certified Specialist - Enterprise Core
Cisco

 Cisco Certified Internetwork Expert Enterprise...
Cisco

 Cisco Certified Internetwork Expert Security (CCIE Security)
Cisco

 Cisco Certified Internetwork Expert Service Provider (CCIE...
Cisco

 Cisco Certified DevNet Associate
Cisco

 DevNet 500
Cisco

---

[1] https://bit.ly/2Pt7R9J

Preface

Congratulations! You have taken your first step towards preparing and passing the Implementing and Administering Cisco Solutions or Cisco Certified Network Associate (CCNA) 200-301 V1.0 Exam.

Did you just purchase a copy? **Interested in getting access to a complimentary CCNA Exam Quiz?** Register here[2] and then send us an email at support@cciein8weeks.com to get started.

This study guide is dedicated to all *those souls who will never settle for less than they can be, do, share, and give!*

---

[2] https://www.cciein8weeks.com/user-account/

What this Study Guide contains

This guide will help you comprehensively prepare for the CCNA exam. As you may already have noticed on the "Contents at a Glance" page that this guide has been formatted around the Cisco's official Network Associate 200-301 official exam topics or curriculum[3]. The benefit? Well, as you read through the various topics, you will know exactly where you're within your learning journey.

All contents are carefully covered with core concepts, configuration and code snippets, and topic summaries to help you master the skills so you can confidently face the pressures of the Cisco exam as well as its real-world application. Cisco networking jargon is going to be uncharted territory for most starters so for this reason, I'd strongly suggest looking up all the terms that appear foreign to you.

---

[3] https://bit.ly/36Q8O1X

How to use this Study Guide

This guide is for anyone who's studying for Cisco Network Associate 200-301 exam. I strongly suggest taking a methodical approach for exam preparation, i.e., start with a target date or when you would like to sit for the actual exam and then work backwards to see what kind of study plan would work for you.

To help further, I have put together a 105-hour learning plan[4] consisting entirely of public resources, something that you can download and follow.

Network Associate CCNA 200-301 V1.0 Exam Topics Bodies of Knowledge	Exam Weight
Network Fundamentals	20%
Network Access	20%
IP Connectivity	25%
IP Services	10%
Security Fundamentals	15%
Automation and Programmability	10%

What's available on the CCIEin8Weeks website

CCIEin8Weeks.com carries the supplemental resources (sold separately) that go hand in hand with this study guide to further ensure your exam success.

- All-in-One CCNA Exam Prep Bundle that covers all concepts and hands-on labs
- 6x Practice Quizzes (one for each section as per the official curriculum)
- 1x Practice Exam simulation (to help you prepare to face the pressure of a real Cisco exam)

---

[4] https://bit.ly/36IOphU

CHAPTER 1 NETWORK FUNDAMENTALS

This chapter covers the following exam topics from Cisco's official 200-901 V1.0[5] Network Associate (CCNA) exam blueprint.

- Explain the role and function of network components
    - Routers
    - L2 and L3 switches
    - Next-generation firewalls and IPS
    - Access points
    - Controllers (Cisco DNA Center and WLC)
    - Endpoints
    - Servers
- Describe characteristics of network topology architectures
    - 2-tier
    - 3-tier
    - Spine-leaf
    - WAN
    - Small office/home office (SOHO)
    - On-premises and cloud
- Compare physical interface and cabling types
    - Single-mode fiber, multimode fiber, copper
    - Connections (Ethernet shared media and point-to-point)
    - Concepts of PoE
- Identify interface and cable issues (collisions, errors, mismatch duplex, and/or speed)
- Compare TCP to UDP
- Configure and verify IPv4 addressing and subnetting
- Describe the need for private IPv4 addressing
- Configure and verify IPv6 addressing and prefix
- Compare IPv6 address types
    - Global unicast

---

[5] https://bit.ly/2PGgv4A

- o Unique local
- o Link local
- o Anycast
- o Multicast
- o Modified EUI 64
- Verify IP parameters for Client OS (Windows, Mac OS, Linux)
- Describe wireless principles
  - o Nonoverlapping Wi-Fi channels
  - o SSID
  - o RF
  - o Encryption
- Explain virtualization fundamentals (virtual machines)
- Describe switching concepts
  - o MAC learning and aging
  - o Frame switching
  - o Frame flooding
  - o MAC address table

Explain the role and function of network components

Routers

Routers route traffic across IP subnets based on the destination IP address or prefix. To facilitate the propagation of routing information, routers also support various routing protocols such as OSPF, EIGRP or BGP.

R1 and R2 are routers connected via an ethernet link.

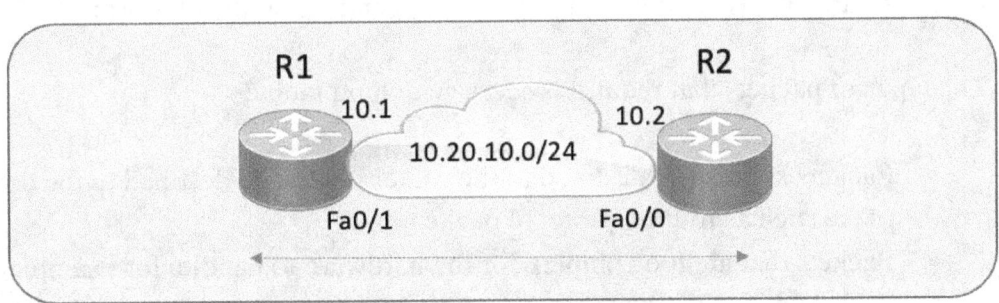

IP packet switching is the process as to how two end hosts communicate with each other. Much like network layer and IP addresses, the data link layer also has its link-layer addresses which are known as MAC addresses for ethernet. If you two end hosts are on the same IP subnet, they do not need a default gateway or a router to communicate with each other. One end-host can use ARP to find out the other's MAC address on an ethernet segment, and then simply transmit the packet to the destination host. However, when the destination host is on a different subnet than the source host, the source host would simply send that packet off to the default gateway or the router. If the router knows how to reach that destination IP subnet, via a static or dynamic routing protocol, the router will simply rewrite the L2 information and send packet off to its destination host using the appropriate outgoing interface.

In the earliest days of networking, Cisco routers switched packets from incoming to outgoing interfaces using process switching which was slow due to the CPU overhead involved. Eventually, Cisco streamlined the process with fast switching and then finally CEF switching.

Process and CEF Switching

Process switching is the switching mechanism in which a general-purpose CPU, e.g. PowerPC or x86 processor, on a router is used to switch packets. In classic IOS, there is an input_process that runs on the CPU for processing all incoming packets. Today, process switching is only limited to a handful of specific scenarios, while everything else gets CEF switched whether in software (i.e. CPU) or hardware (i.e. network processor) depending on the platform.

The types of packets that require process switching include

- Packets sourced or destined to the router i.e. traffic destined to the control plane such as routing protocol packets
- Packets that are too complex for the hardware to handle, for example, packets with IP options set
- Packets that require extra information such as ARP resolution etc.

The routing table, also known as Routing Information Base (or RIB) is built from information gained from either directly connected interfaces and/or static or dynamic routing protocols.

Cisco Express Forwarding (or CEF) is a Cisco proprietary switching method developed back in the 1990s to keep pace with the modern high capacity and low latency networks. Today, it is the default switching method across all Cisco routers, switches, and even appliances. CEF can be done in software or hardware. CEF can be implemented on both centralized (e.g. ISR 4K or ASR1K) as well as the distributed (e.g. Cisco ASR9K or Nexus 7K) forwarding platforms. Please note that concepts of centralized and distributed forwarding are orthogonal to whether a platform is software-based or hardware.

Software-based CEF

Software-based CEF implies CEF processing done using a general-purpose processor as opposed to using an ASIC or a network processor. CEF consists of two major components, i.e. Forwarding Information Base (or FIB) and Adjacency table.

The FIB is built directly from the routing table and contains next-hop IP addresses for each destination IP prefix. It is updated when a routing or topology change occurs.

Adjacency table contains MAC addresses and egress interfaces of all directly connected next hops and is populated using the ARP table (for ethernet medium).

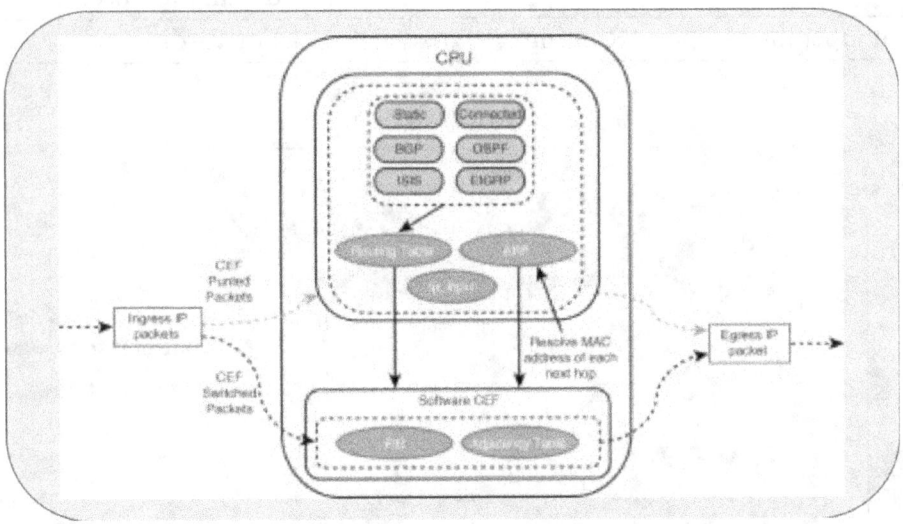

Hardware-based CEF

Hardware-based CEF is where forwarding is done with the help of ASIC(s) or network processor(s). It can be either centralized (e.g. ASR1K) or distributed (e.g. ASR9K or CRS-1).

The primary advantage of distributed forwarding is that the packet throughput is improved even more so by offloading forwarding tasks to the egress line card(s).

FIB vs. RIB

FIB is used for forwarding but is derived from the combination of RIB and adjacency table so that L2 information in each outgoing frame can be rewritten.

	RIB	**FIB**
Architecture	IP routing table (best AD only)	CEF table
Data Structure	Repository of routes	Repository of interface IDs and next-hop information for each destination prefix
Plane of Operation	Routing	Forwarding

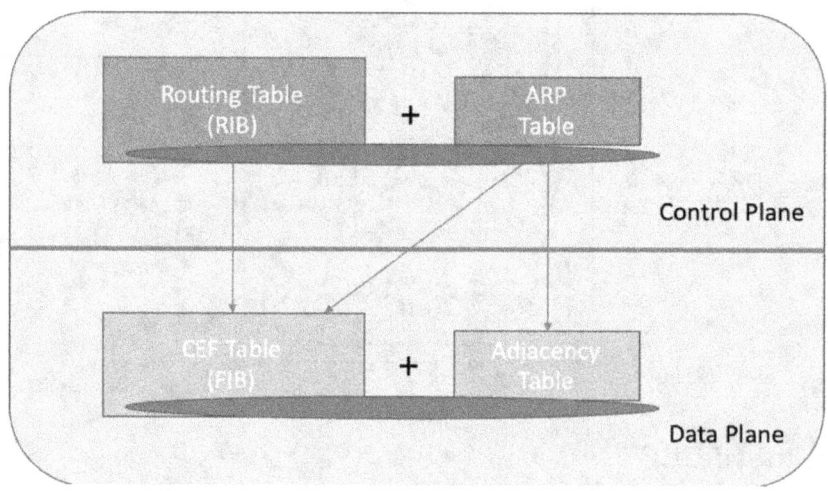

The RIB can be local to a routing protocol such as the case with the OSPFv2[6]. The OSPFv2 local RIB acts as the primary state management data structure for

---
[6] https://bit.ly/2ScHxkS

SPF computation which minimizes the churn within the global RIB and leads to lesser packet drops. The global RIB is updated only when routes are added, deleted or changed. By default, the global RIB is used to compute inter-area, NSSA and forwarding addresses for type 5 and 7 LSAs.

L2 and L3 switches

L2 Switches are for bridging or forwarding traffic based on the destination MAC address within a given L2 segment or VLAN based on CAM table which is built using the source MAC addresses. L3 switches can function both as an L2 switch as well as a router for inter-VLAN routing and many other use cases. Cisco Nexus 3000, 5000, 7000, and 9000 series products represent layer 3 family of switches.

The following steps describe the switching process.

- The switch receives a frame from a source machine
- The switch stores the source MAC address and the switch port that the frame was received on into the MAC table.
- The switch checks the table for the matching destination MAC address. If there is a match, that port is used to forward the frame. If there is no match, it is flooded out of all the switch ports (for that VLAN).

Next-generation firewalls and IPS

Firewalls can be divided into several types based on how they operate on traffic passing through them. The actual implementation could be in the form of a physical or virtual appliance, the latter also suitable for cloud deployments.

- Packet filters (or stateless FW such as an ACL)
- Stateful FW (such as IOS ZBFW or Cisco ASA without any AVC, APM, etc. configured)
- Application-layer firewalls (e.g. proxies)

- Next-gen firewalls (e.g. Cisco Firepower with application-level controls)
- Cloud firewalls (mostly virtual appliances, OVAs)

It is worth noting that there is no consensus or a definition of what a next-gen firewall is in the security industry. There are two main ways a firewall can be deployed in an enterprise network.

- Firewall as bastion host (you can also call this two-legged deployment where a FW separates the trusted from the untrusted network). This is the single most common deployment model.
- Firewall as bastion host with DMZ (this is your three-legged deployment where a FW has a third connection facing the servers (such as web, mail and DNS)

In the case of a firewall as a bastion host with DMZ, you can also choose to deploy two separate firewalls, one facing the trusted (or private) and the other facing the untrusted or public network. Servers on the DMZ are only allowed to send traffic in response to traffic coming from the hosts on the trusted or untrusted network. The biggest drawback associated with a traditional FW deployment is that it does nothing to prevent attacks coming from the inside the network.

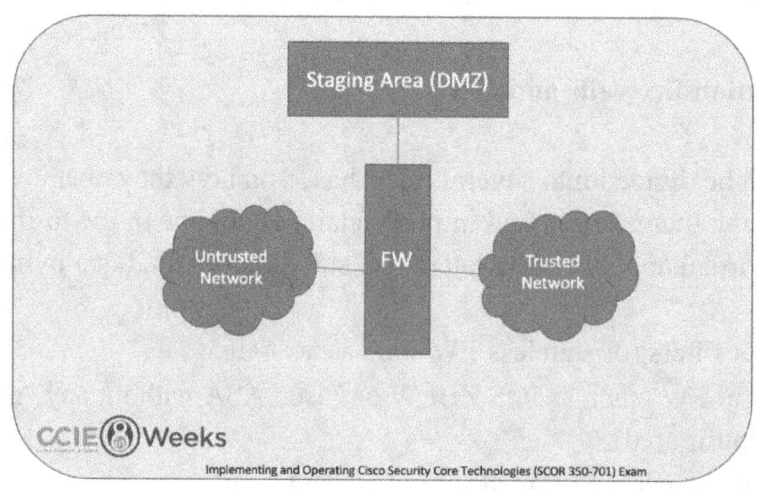

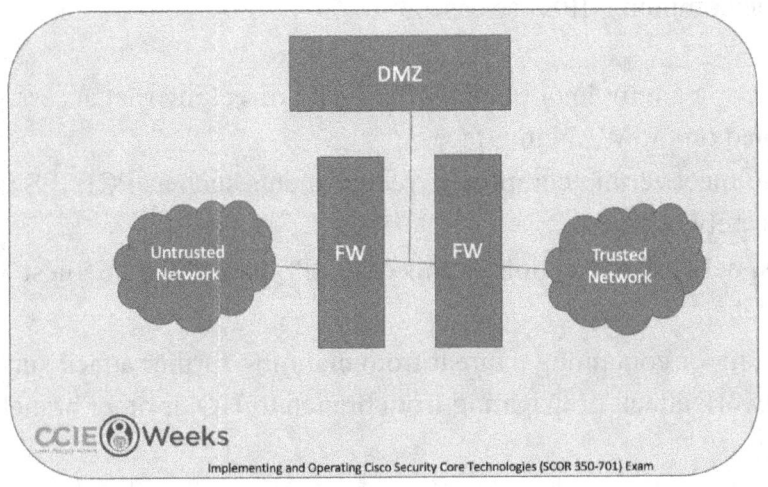

Intrusion Prevention Systems (IPS) systems come in a variety of shapes and forms, below are the four most common ones.

- Network-based IPS (or NIPS, protect the traffic behind it)
- Host-based IPS (or HIPS protect the computer or host it is installed on)
- Wireless IPS (or WIPS only monitors WLAN traffic)
- Network Behavior Analysis (or NBA, looks at unusual traffic pattern or volume such as the case with DDoS)

IPS is deployed alongside firewall clusters, and its placement depends on the underlying use case. IPS can be deployed either in an in-line or TAP (aka passive) mode. In an in-line deployment, all network traffic passes through the IPS, and the ports can be configured in a fail-closed (i.e., no traffic passes if port or the IPS malfunctions) or fail-open fashion.

In a passive IPS deployment, an IPS such as a Firepower system monitors traffic flowing across a network using a switch port that's configured for port mirroring or SPAN. The SPAN port receives all traffic data copied from other ports, so this type of deployment allows for placing the IPS just about anywhere within the L2 domain. In passive mode, an IPS cannot take actions that require it to be in the data path, such as blocking or shaping.

Below are the common NIPS use cases.

- Protecting a remote or branch office with direct internet access. IPS is enabled on the WAN interface.
- IPS to meet certain compliance requirements such as PCI. IPS is placed at the network edge.
- Guest network protection, in this case, IPS is enabled on guest VLAN interface.
- Limiting or containing a threat from claiming further attack surface, e.g. a network attack propagating from branch to HQ or other branches.

Access points

Cisco WLAN infrastructure consists of either autonomous (standalone) or lightweight APs (LAPs) that are connected to the network via WLAN controllers. The autonomous APs are also known as Fat APs.

Controllers (Cisco DNA Center and WLC)

A Wireless LAN (WLAN) controller manages wireless network access points (APs) that wireless devices use to connect to the wireless network. WLAN controller can be deployed in a centralized (most common) or distributed fashion.

Cisco's WLAN controllers are a key component of intent-based networking. Cisco DNA center is a controller as well as an analytics platform that makes Cisco's intent-based networking possible. It consists of five major components.

- Design
- Policy
- Provision
- Assurance

DNA center appliance hosts SDN controller, analytics engine and telemetry storage. At the time of writing, a 44-core DNA appliance (DN2-HW-APL) is listed for USD 88.6K in Cisco's GPL. It must be installed and run on the bundled bare metal server, as we speak, there is no virtual appliance package available.

DNA center licenses come in three flavors, i.e.

- Essentials (includes basic automation and network visibility)
- Advantage (includes Essentials, plus advanced automation, image lifecycle management, AI/ML analytics and assurance and API/SDK integration)
- Premier (Everything in Advantage, plus encrypted traffic analytics and multi-domain policy segmentation)

Endpoints

Endpoints are desktop or mobile clients that connect into networks to consume network services and access resources. For example, a network connected laptop, desktop, smartphone, tablets, printers or any other network connected hardware with a TCP/IP stack.

Servers

A server is a hardware of software device on a network that accepts and responds to a network connection request made by a client or an endpoint. Servers are purpose-built computers to carry out various network functions. For example, a web server is a computer that runs web services (i.e. Apache or Microsoft IIS software) and responds to HTTP/HTTPS requests coming in from the web clients.

Describe characteristics of network topology architectures

The network is simply a resource, and a means to an end, thus every enterprise network is laid out to facilitate the applications running on top of it. The network will meet its goals if enterprise applications can run in a reliable and performant manner. With the increasing adoption of cloud applications (or SaaS apps such as CRM or HRM), i.e., applications that are hosted by the providers (such as Salesforce) in their own data centers as opposed to being on-premise, the role of the network changes again.

In the new world of cloud apps, the network still has to provide reliable and performant access to those off-premise apps, but even more so maintain the necessary user experience, security, compliance and visibility and control with the help of solutions such as Cloud Access Security Broker (or CASB[7]).

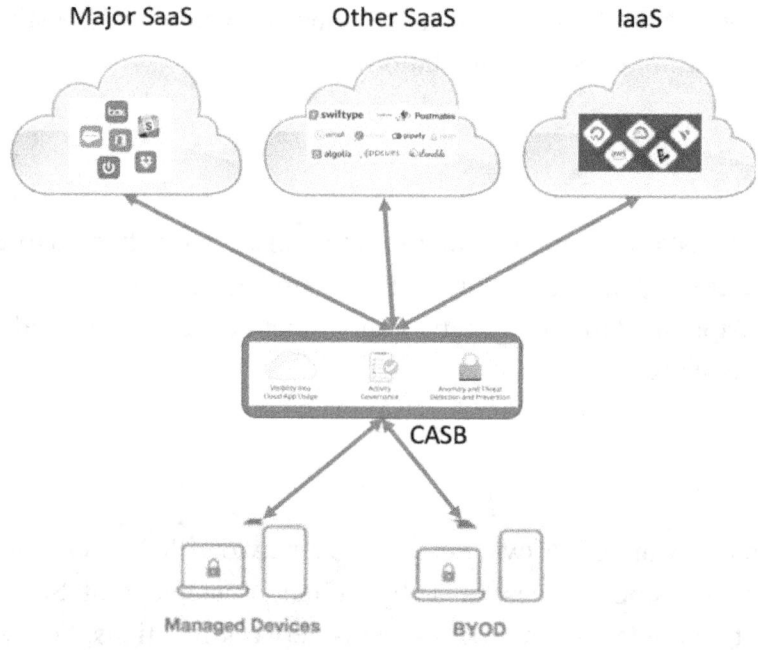

While you've to build your network for current requirements, it must be able to evolve, for example where your core design choices stay the same (for example, 2-tier versus 3-tier architecture), so think in a modular fashion. Still, at the same time, other parts of the network can evolve, much like building blocks of a Lego. Whether you are designing for only on-premise or everything off-prem

---

[7] https://en.wikipedia.org/wiki/Cloud_access_security_broker

(SaaS/PaaS), you are design will still need to be performant, resilient, and scalable.

Enterprise campus network can span over a single building or a group of buildings spread out over a large geographic area much like a college campus but still in closer proximity. The primary goal of the campus design is to deliver the fastest speed (say 1 or 10 Gbps) and variety of access (LAN, WLAN) options to the endpoints.

Campus network design can be organized around four core principles, i.e.

- Hierarchy (2-tier / 2-layer or 3-tier / 3-layer)
- Modularity (functional building blocks, collection of devices within a layer)
- Resiliency
- Flexibility

In 1999, Cisco pioneered the campus network design with hierarchical design model which used a layered approach. The hierarchical network design can help break down otherwise complex and flat networks into multiple smaller and manageable network tiers or layers. Each layer is focused on a specific set of requirements and roles. With this design, network designers can pick the most suitable platform and software features for each layer. As we discussed earlier, regardless of how a network was designed, the ability to modify an existing design, i.e. without rip and replace, is of utmost importance. There can be many underlying reasons for such modifications, i.e. addition of newer services, more bandwidth, and so on.

2-tier

Two-layer design is a modified three-layer design where the core has been collapsed into the distribution layer. The main motivation for the collapsed core has to do with cost and the operational simplicity that it brings. It is best suited for small to medium-sized networks.

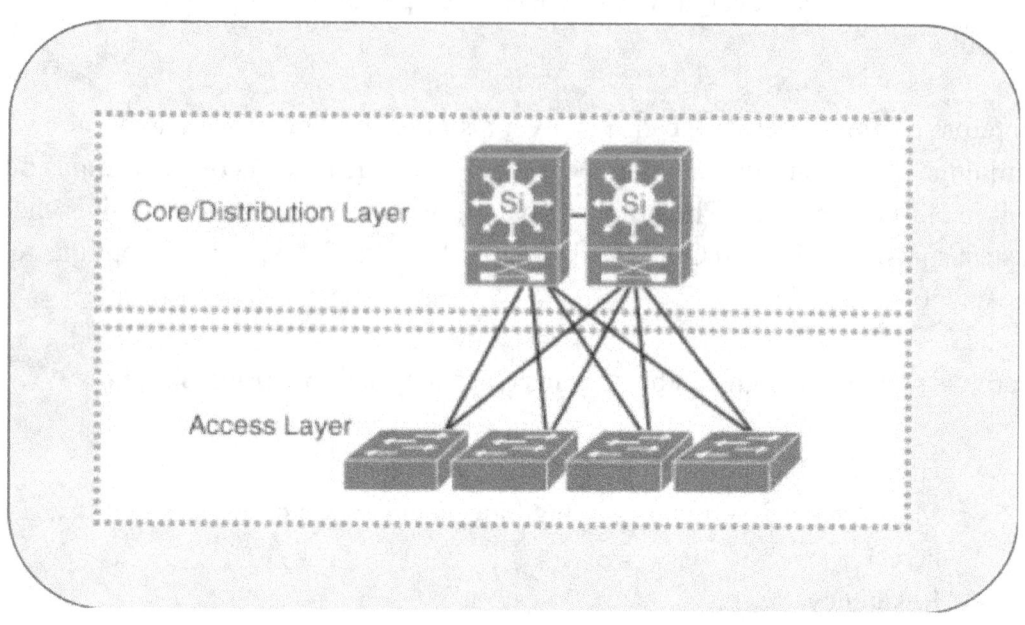

It is worth noting that the above discussion is about enterprise campus design and not enterprise data center. The campus is where end-users connect to the network whereas the data center provides connectivity to the servers and devices such as load balancers and storage arrays. Let's now summarize the key differences between the two network designs before we move on.

	Campus Network	**Data Center Network**
Architecture	Three or two-tier	Three-tier or Leaf-Spine Clos
Traffic Flow	Mostly North-South	North-South and East-West (depending on the applications)
Speeds and Feeds	Mostly 1G for access and 10/40G for uplinks	Mostly 10/40G for access and 10/40/100G for uplinks
Oversubscription	Typically, 20:1	Typically, 1:1 or 4:1
Failure domains	Mostly limited impact	Mostly larger impact
Access Medium	Wired and Wireless	Wired only

3-tier

When you think of network design, you're likely thinking about the most discussed and much talked about three tier or three-layer design. The three-layer design is most suited to large enterprise campus networks. Those three layers are:

1. Core
2. Distribution
3. Access

Now, let's go over the primary functions of each layer.

- Core layer provides transport between distribution layer devices.
- Distribution layer provides policy driven connectivity and boundary control between the access and core layers. It is the boundary between the layer 2 and layer 3 domains.
- Access layer provides users access to the network

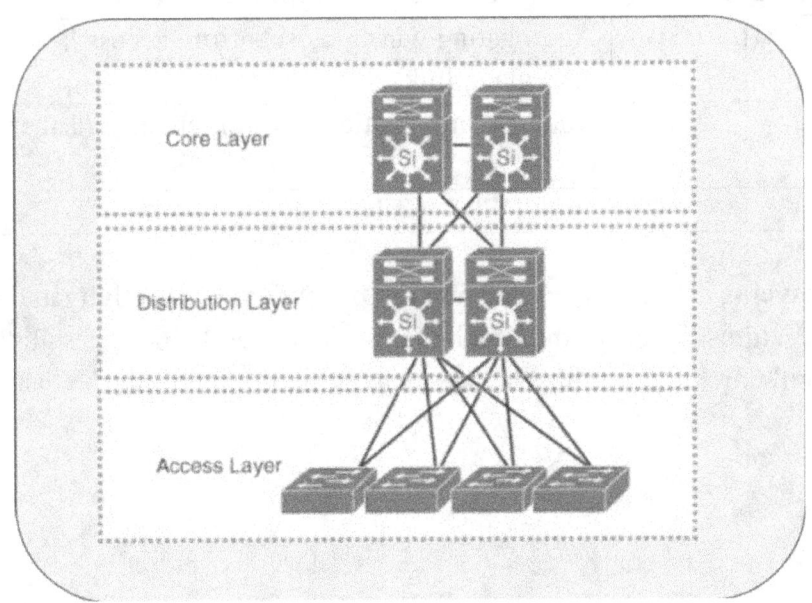

Each layer in the 3-tier architecture provides a distinct function and thus relies on a unique set of features. The access layer is not just about connectivity but also feature richness up and down the OSI stack.

OSI Layer	Typical Access Layer Features
L1-L2 (convergence, HA, security, multicast)	PVST+, Rapid PVST+, LACP, UDLD, FlexLink, IGMP Snooping, PoE, DHCP Snooping, DAI, IPSG, Port Security, broadcast suppression, Aux VLAN, 802.1x, PortFast, UplinkFast, BackboneFast, LoopGuard, BPDU Guard, BPDU Filter, RootGuard, DTP, etc.
L3 (convergence, HA, security, multicast)	EIGRP, OSPF, IP multicast
IP Services	QoS

The distribution layer is about the connectivity as well as policy, convergence, QoS and HA features.

OSI Layer	Typical Distribution Layer Features
Connectivity (L2/L3)	Aggregating wiring closets from access layer to the core via uplinks
L3	Route summarization, convergence, load sharing, etc.
IP Services	QoS, HSRP, GLBP, etc.

The core layer is about high speed and high bandwidth connectivity and less about the features. It acts as the backbone for the network and glues all the network building blocks. It also acts as an aggregation point for the distribution layer.

Spine-leaf

Leaf-spine or spine-leaf is a two-layer network topology composed of leaf and spine switches. Leaf switches mesh into the spine switches forming the access layer that acts as the network connection points for the servers.

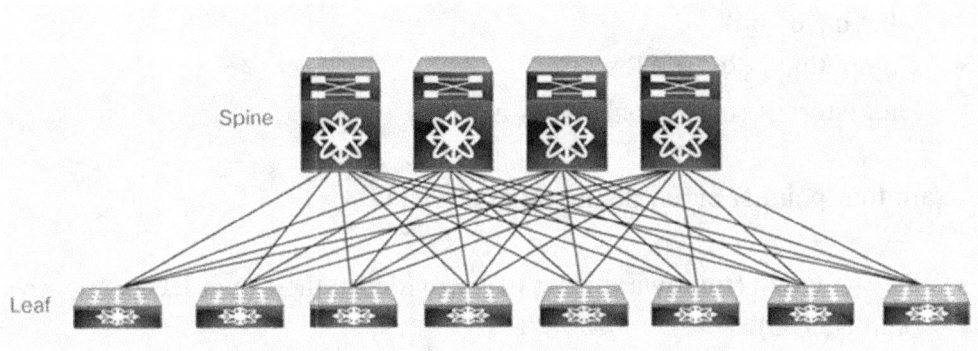

WAN

Wide Area Network (WAN) is a network connectivity medium that spans a large geographical area. WANs allow remote branch offices to connect into the enterprise HQ.

Small office/home office (SOHO)

SOHO refers to a small office or home office that typically has less than 10 employees.

On-premises and cloud

As cloud adoption picked up, purchasing and maintaining on-premise infrastructure went from being an investment to a liability. While cloud and on-premise are two different deployment models, but behind the scene, enterprises still have a singular goal of implementing a lean and agile IT infrastructure that meets or exceeds a company's needs while optimizing the cost. There are three major types of infrastructure, or raw material if you like, that can be deployed on-premise or used in the cloud, i.e.

- Networking infrastructure (routers, switches, firewalls, load balancers what have you)
- Computing (x86 or ARM)
- Data Storage (traditional arrays or HCI)

There are four popular cloud deployment models.

- Private cloud (run by a third-party provider in their own DC or within on-premise DC)
- Public cloud (run by a third-party provider in their own DC)
- Hybrid cloud (mix of public and private cloud)
- Multi-cloud (mix of various public clouds, private cloud is not mandatory)

Compare physical interface and cabling types

Single-mode fiber, multimode fiber, copper

Fiber or fiber-optic is a strand of transparent glass as thing as a human hair that is used to carry digital transmission over long distances. There are two main types of fiber optic cables in use today, i.e. single and multimode fiber.

Single mode (SMF) means the fiber enables one type of light mode to be propagated at a time, whereas multimode (MMF) means that the fiber can propagate multiple modes. The actual difference between single versus multimode fiber cable is about the fiber core diameter, wavelength and light source, bandwidth, color sheath, distance and cost.

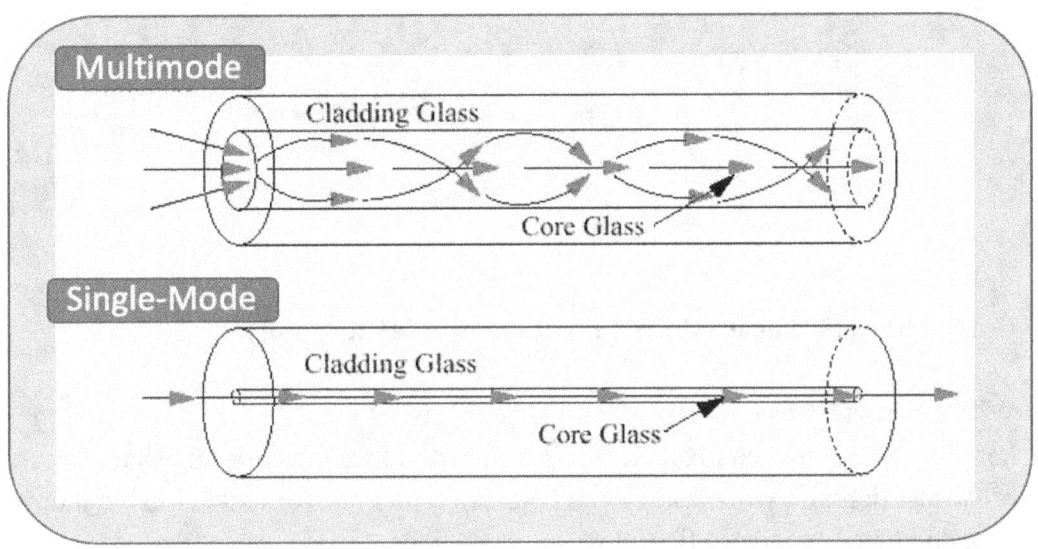

Copper cable uses electrical, as opposed to light, to pass data between networks. There are three types of copper cables in use today for data transmission, i.e. shielded twisted pair (STP), unshielded twisted pair (UTP), and coaxial. Coaxial cables are not suitable for data transmission over long distances. Unshielded twisted pair is made by twisting the copper cables around each other to reduce signal degradation.

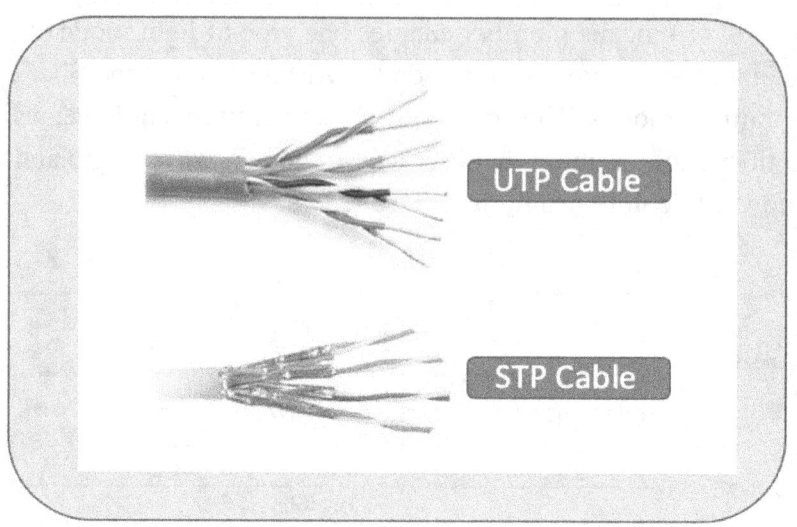

Connections (Ethernet shared media and point-to-point)

With ethernet, shared refers to a broadcast channel where every transmission is heard by all connected hosts. Devices connected to a network hub share one broadcast domain, whereas devices connected to a network switch have their own dedicated broadcast domains.

Concepts of PoE

Power over Ethernet (PoE) describes a mechanism where power is passed along with data on a twister pair ethernet cabling. There are many applications for PoE, but the most common ones include IP camera, access points, and VoIP phones.

PoE provides several benefits for ethernet installation.

- Time and cost savings: Network cable carry both data and power, thus eliminating need for a separate power cable and a qualified electrician to install them.
- Location flexibility: Devices such as IP camera or access points can be located anywhere i.e. without being tethered to a power outlet.

- Safety: PoE delivery is intelligent and protects equipment from general power issues.
- Reliability: PoE power comes from a single source and that makes it possible for it to be centrally backed up by a UPS.

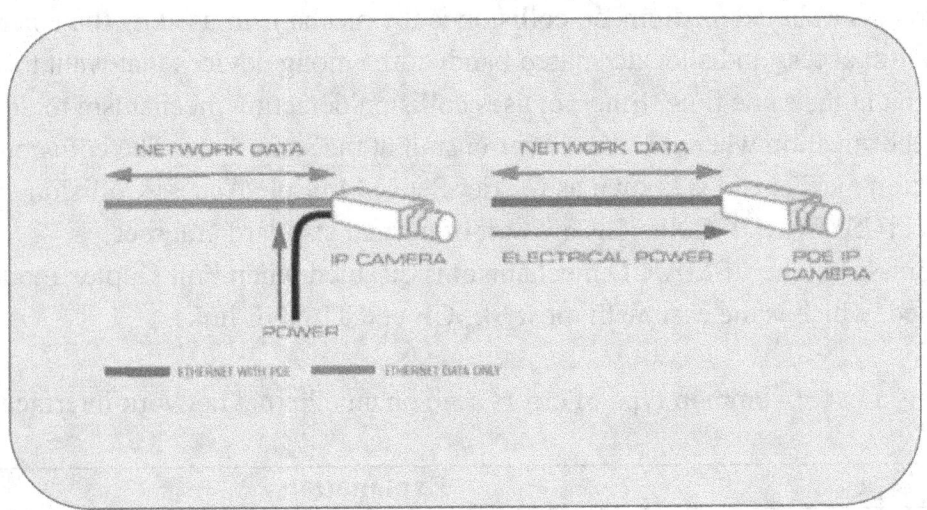

There are three main standards for PoE today.

- IEEE 802.2af: This is the original PoE standard and it provides up to 15.4W of power. The devices that support this standard are known as Type 1 devices.
- IEEE 802.3at or PoE+: PoE plus is the revised PoE standard which can provide up to 30W of power. The devices that supports PoE plus are known as Type 2 devices.
- IEEE 802.3bt: This is the most recent PoE standard and provides even higher power levels. The devices that support this standard can provide up to 55W (Type 3) and up to 100W (Type 4). This standard also brings PoE to higher bandwidth ethernet, i.e. 2.5Gbps, 5Gbps and 10Gbps.

PoE standards define two types of devices, i.e. power sourcing equipment (PSE) and powered devices (PD). PSE (a power injector or a switch) is a device that supplies the power, whereas PD is the device receiving the power such as a VOIP phone or remote IP camera.

Identify interface and cable issues (collisions, errors, mismatch duplex, and/or speed)

Ethernet is a shared medium, so collision is the mechanism used by the ethernet to control access and allocate shared bandwidth among devices that want to transmit at the same time. Ethernet uses collision detection mechanism to deal with the situation where two stations transmit at the same time. The collision detection mechanism is known as Carrier Sense Multiple Access/Collision Detect (CSMA/CD). Collisions are part of normal standard ethernet transmission. The CSMA/CD mechanism is disabled when Full Duplex mode is enabled, which is the case with most FE, GE and TENGE links.

Here is a list of common type of errors seen on an ethernet network interface.

Type	Explanation
Runt	This is a frame that is shorter than 64 bytes.
Giant	This is a frame that is longer than 6000 bytes long.
FCS/CRC Error	When a frame is corrupted during transmission, the resulting error is known as FCS or CRC.
Collisions	Collision occurs when two or more stations try to transmit at the same time. Late collision occurs when two devices transmit at the same time without detecting a collision. If a device attempts to transmit 16 times without success, then that situation is known as excessive collision. In case of excessive collisions, no transmission is attempted.
Jam	When a collision is detected in half-duplex networks, the ethernet network interface sends out a Jam signal to let the other stations know that a collision has occurred.

In ethernet, the two stations must use the same duplex, half/half or full/full. However, if two stations have mismatching duplexes then the situation is formally known as duplex mismatch and leads to inefficient operation. You are likely to see runts and/or excess collisions.

If the two links are set to different speeds (say 10Mbps and 100Mbps), then the link will not fully come up.

Compare TCP to UDP

Transmission Control Protocol (TCP) and User Data Protocol (UDP) are two transport protocols for the IP stack.

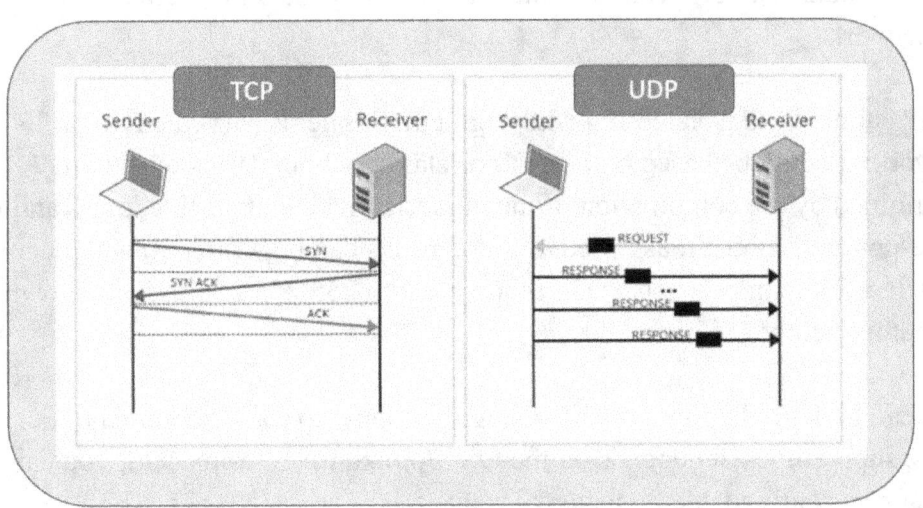

TCP	UDP
Connection-oriented	Connection-less
Reliable	Unreliable (no guaranteed delivery or retransmission)
Flow control	No flow control
Ordered delivery	No ordered delivery
Slower (due to connection, error checking and guaranteed delivery)	Faster (best effort delivery)
HTTP/HTTPS, SSH, FTP, SMTP,	DNS, VoIP, TFTP, multicasts

IMAP/POP	

Configure and verify IPv4 addressing and subnetting

IP address is a numerical label assigned to each endpoint that is connected to a network that uses Internet Protocol (or IP). There are two variants of IP labels and protocols, one that's known as IPv4 and the other one that's known as IPv6. IPv4 and IPv6 address spaces are 32-bit and 128-bit long.

In IP nomenclature, a route is a way to reach another IP destination or a prefix. Routing is done hop-by-hop in an IP network, thus for each prefix, one or more next-hop addresses are what's needed to reach beyond an IP network or subnetwork.

An IP subnet is an isolated IP or L3 segment. Subnet is carved out of an IP network; it could be based on classful or classless boundaries which are determined by the combination of the numerical value of an IP address and the corresponding subnet mask used. Subnet masks can be written in both decimals as well as bit lengths, such as /32 (equivalent to 255.255.255.255) as shown in the output below.

You can look up the routing table using the "show ip route" command. For end hosts, such as PCs, it depends on the OS. For example, for macOS, you can view the current routing table by using "netstat -rn".

```
MAK1-MBP:~ afaqkhan$ netstat -rn
Routing tables

Internet:
Destination        Gateway              Flags       Netif Expire
default            192.168.1.1          UGSc        en0
127                127.0.0.1            UCS         lo0
127.0.0.1          127.0.0.1            UH          lo0
169.254            link#5               UCS         en0      !
192.168.1          link#5               UCS         en0      !
192.168.1.1/32     link#5               UCS         en0      !
192.168.1.1        14:91:82:96:1d:a5    UHLWIir     en0     1171
192.168.1.12/32    link#5               UCS         en0      !
192.168.1.28       c4:95:0:9a:52:9      UHLWI       en0     1199
192.168.1.59       0:80:92:d5:2e:c3     UHLWI       en0     1150
192.168.1.86       f8:38:80:67:5c:71    UHLWIi      en0     1153
192.168.1.130      ac:cf:5c:ac:f4:39    UHLWI       en0      !
192.168.1.173      14:91:82:95:a0:e3    UHLWI       en0     1167
192.168.1.227      c4:1c:ff:25:f3:8e    UHLWIi      en0     181
192.168.1.247      14:20:5e:c2:24:f1    UHLWIi      en0     1104
224.0.0/4          link#5               UmCS        en0      !
224.0.0.251        1:0:5e:0:0:fb        UHmLWI      en0
255.255.255.255/32 link#5               UCS         en0      !
```

Gateway or default gateway, typical a router or an L3 switch, is a special type of IP address, which allows a host from one subnet to send traffic to another subnet or the internet itself (i.e. networks for which your gateway doesn't know of). In the example above, 192.168.1.1 is the default gateway IP address for en0.

There are five classes of IP addresses.

Class	Network bits	Host bits	Subnet mask
A	8	24	255.0.0.0
B	16	16	255.255.0.0
C	24	8	255.255.255.0
D	Reserved	Reserved	n/a
E	Reserved	Reserved	n/a

Describe the need for private IPv4 addressing

Private IP networks, as opposed to their public counterpart, are not allocated to any specific organization. They were created to conserve globally unique IP addresses. Both IPv4 and IPv6 address families define their private IP address ranges in RFC 1918 and RFC 4193 respectively.

Here is a snapshot of the projected availability of the IPv4 address free pool in each Regional Internet Registry (RIR) as of December 2019.

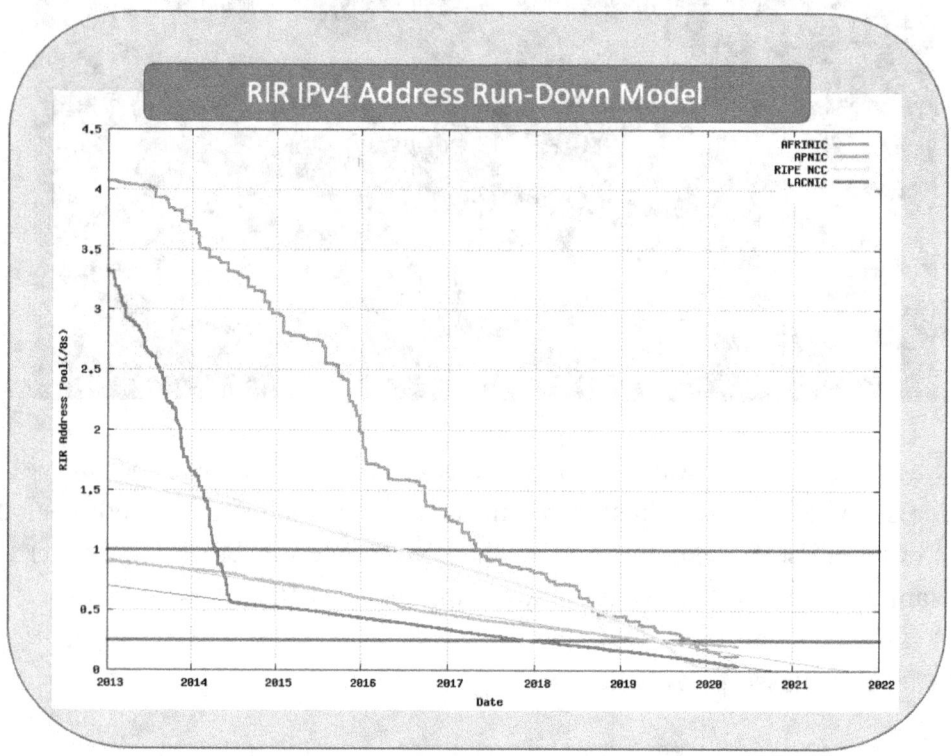

As per the RFC 1918, here are the main reasons for private IPv4 addressing.

- To slow down the eventual globally unique IPv4 address space exhaustion
- To allow enterprises to go online without needing many public IP addresses (NAT/PAT and default routing are enough)

| Address class | RFC 1918 Address space | Total # of |

		Addresses
Single Class A network (24-bit block)	10.0.0.0 to 10.255.255.255	16.7M
16 contiguous Class B networks (20-bit block)	172.16.0.0 to 172.31.255.255	1M
256 contiguous class C networks (16-bit block)	192.168.0.0 to 192.168.255.255	65K

Configure and verify IPv6 addressing and prefix

IPv6 address space expands the number of address bits from 32-bit (in IPv4) to 128-bit. The larger address space provides more globally unique addresses and help deal with the IPv4 address exhaustion.

IPv6 addresses are represented as 16-bit hexadecimal fields separated by colons.

2001:DB8:7654:3210:FCDE:BA98:7654:0001

A double colon may be used as part of the IPv6 address when consecutive 16-bit values are denoted as zero. For example, you can write 2001:0:0:0:DB8:800:200C:4ABC as 2001::DB8:800:200C:4ABC.

Router(config-if)# ipv6 address 2001:DB8:0:1::/64 eui-64
Router(config-if)#ipv6 unicast-routing
Router(config-if)#ipv6 enable

You can verify the configured address by using "show ipv6 interface gigabitethernet" command.

Router# show ipv6 interface gigabitethernet 0/0/0
Gigabitethernet0/0/0 is up, line protocol is up
 IPv6 is enabled, link-local address is FE80::260:3EFF:FE47:1530
  Global unicast address(es):
   2001:DB8:C18:1:260:3EFF:FE47:1530, subnet is 2001:DB8:C18:1::/64

```
  Joined group address(es):
    FF02::1
    FF02::2
    FF02::1:FF47:1530
    FF02::9
  MTU is 1500 bytes
  ICMP error messages limited to one every 500 milliseconds
  ND reachable time is 30000 milliseconds
  ND advertised reachable time is 0 milliseconds
  ND advertised retransmit interval is 0 milliseconds
  ND router advertisements are sent every 200 seconds
  ND router advertisements live for 1800 seconds
  Hosts use stateless autoconfig for addresses.
```

Compare IPv6 address types

There are three main types of IPv6 addresses, namely unicast (single interface), multicast (set of interfaces), and anycast (set of interfaces). Unicast addresses can be further divided into

Global unicast

It is a unique IPv6 address assigned to a host interface. As the name implies, these addresses have a global scope and thus like globally routable public IPv4 addresses. These addresses are routable on the Internet.

Unique local

A unique local address (ULA) is like an RFC 1918 private IPv4 address. The address block FC00::/7 is reserved for ULAs.

Link local

It is an IPv6 address that allows communication between neighboring hosts that reside on the same link. Link local addresses have a local scope and thus cannot be used outside the link. Link local addresses are prefixed with FE80::/10.

Anycast

Anycast addresses are like multicast addresses except that packets are received by only one interface. The routing protocol used determines which interface is physically closest within the set of anycast addresses and routes packets to its destination.

Multicast

Much like IPv4, an IPv6 multicast address defines a group of endpoints known as the multicast group. IPv6 multicast addresses use the FF00::/8 prefix which is equivalent to IPv4 224.0.0.0/4 multicast address.

Modified EUI 64

Modified EUI-64 is the process that allows a host to assign itself a unique IPv6 address. The host MAC address is converted into a 64-bit identifier and is combined with another 64-bit network prefix. If you recall, a MAC address comprises of two 24-bit fields (or 48-bit total) in length so that requires adding another 16-bit (reserved value of FFFE) to construct a 64-bit identifier.

This contrasts with IPv4 where acquiring an IP address either happens via DHCP or manual configuration.

Verify IP parameters for Client OS (Windows, Mac OS, Linux)

You can use "ip config" to view IP configuration for all your network interfaces.

```
C:\Users\varma>ipconfig

Windows IP Configuration

Ethernet adapter Local Area Connection:

   Connection-specific DNS Suffix  . : local.lan
   Link-local IPv6 Address . . . . . : fe80::e4d7:ad1e:37b7:fca%11
   IPv4 Address. . . . . . . . . . . : 192.168.1.12
   Subnet Mask . . . . . . . . . . . : 255.255.255.0
   Default Gateway . . . . . . . . . : fe80::225:5eff:fe54:8a27%11
                                       192.168.1.1

Tunnel adapter isatap.local.lan:

   Media State . . . . . . . . . . . : Media disconnected
   Connection-specific DNS Suffix  . : local.lan

Tunnel adapter Local Area Connection* 11:

   Connection-specific DNS Suffix  . :
   IPv6 Address. . . . . . . . . . . : 2001:0:4137:9e76:f6:3ce2:8a3b:988f
   Link-local IPv6 Address . . . . . : fe80::f6:3ce2:8a3b:988f%12
```

For macOS and Linux, you can use "ifconfig" to view IP configuration parameters.

```
MAK1-MBP:~ afaqkhan$ ifconfig | grep inet
        inet 127.0.0.1 netmask 0xff000000
        inet6 ::1 prefixlen 128
        inet6 fe80::1%lo0 prefixlen 64 scopeid 0x1
        inet6 fe80::cac:3d25:5af3:e474%en0 prefixlen 64 secured scopeid 0x5
        inet 192.168.1.12 netmask 0xffffff00 broadcast 192.168.1.255
        inet6 fe80::98a7:4dff:fe15:cd09%awdl0 prefixlen 64 scopeid 0x7
        inet6 fe80::98a7:4dff:fe15:cd09%llw0 prefixlen 64 scopeid 0x8
        inet6 fe80::cf46:d1f7:3c4a:8fcf%utun0 prefixlen 64 scopeid 0xe
        inet6 fe80::9435:7c01:4021:bb60%utun1 prefixlen 64 scopeid 0xf
        inet6 fe80::4ca5:b4c3:d55a:3401%utun2 prefixlen 64 scopeid 0x11
        inet6 fe80::6370:bbd1:8e8b:3ed0%utun3 prefixlen 64 scopeid 0x12
        inet6 fe80::2144:ddee:6205:929c%utun4 prefixlen 64 scopeid 0x13
        inet6 fe80::4309:e6d6:69c2:3e5c%utun5 prefixlen 64 scopeid 0x14
        inet6 fe80::217d:a55b:822d:b8af%utun6 prefixlen 64 scopeid 0x15
        inet6 fe80::ea7f:8c16:d83:d28e%utun7 prefixlen 64 scopeid 0x16
        inet6 fe80::dea9:4ff:fe7c:7ae7%ipsec0 prefixlen 64 scopeid 0x10
        inet6 2607:fb90:5c3:18c8:dd5a:b3c2:91bb:5b32 prefixlen 64
        inet6 fe80::aede:48ff:fe00:1122%en5 prefixlen 64 scopeid 0x4
```

```
😐😐😐    ubuntu@ubuntu: ~
ubuntu@ubuntu:~$ ifconfig
eth0      Link encap:Ethernet  HWaddr 00:0c:29:3c:73:32
          inet6 addr: fe80::20c:29ff:fe3c:7332/64 Scope:Link
          UP BROADCAST RUNNING MULTICAST  MTU:1500  Metric:1
          RX packets:0 errors:0 dropped:0 overruns:0 frame:0
          TX packets:94 errors:0 dropped:0 overruns:0 carrier:0
          collisions:0 txqueuelen:1000
          RX bytes:0 (0.0 B)  TX bytes:20948 (20.9 KB)

lo        Link encap:Local Loopback
          inet addr:127.0.0.1  Mask:255.0.0.0
          inet6 addr: ::1/128 Scope:Host
          UP LOOPBACK RUNNING  MTU:16436  Metric:1
          RX packets:16 errors:0 dropped:0 overruns:0 frame:0
          TX packets:16 errors:0 dropped:0 overruns:0 carrier:0
          collisions:0 txqueuelen:0
          RX bytes:1312 (1.3 KB)  TX bytes:1312 (1.3 KB)
```

Describe wireless principles

Nonoverlapping Wi-Fi channels

Wireless is an air interface and thus a shared medium. Interference in a wireless network occurs when a signal as transmitted by one device gets disrupted in transit to the receiving device. As you can expect, all interference result in performance degradation.

There are two types of interference when it comes to Wi-Fi, one that's caused by non-Wi-Fi sources and ones caused by Wi-Fi sources (other wireless routers or access points). If you've so much interference or noise caused by Wi-Fi devices that no one can receive a signal, that phenomenon is known as co-channel interface or CCI. CCI is about everyone trying to use same frequency in the given space.

Adjacent channel interference (or ACI) is when transmissions are sent on an adjacent or partially overlapping channel. ACI occurs as a result of bleed over to an overlapping channel which causes noise and interference. In practice, ACI is much worse than CCI.

SSID

In IEEE 802.11 WLAN standard, the Service Set Identifier (SSID) is a fancy word for the network or Wi-Fi name. When you set up a new WLAN, you pick up a unique name to differentiate it from other existing WLANs.

On macOS, you can view your currently used SSID by going to the System Preferences > Network.

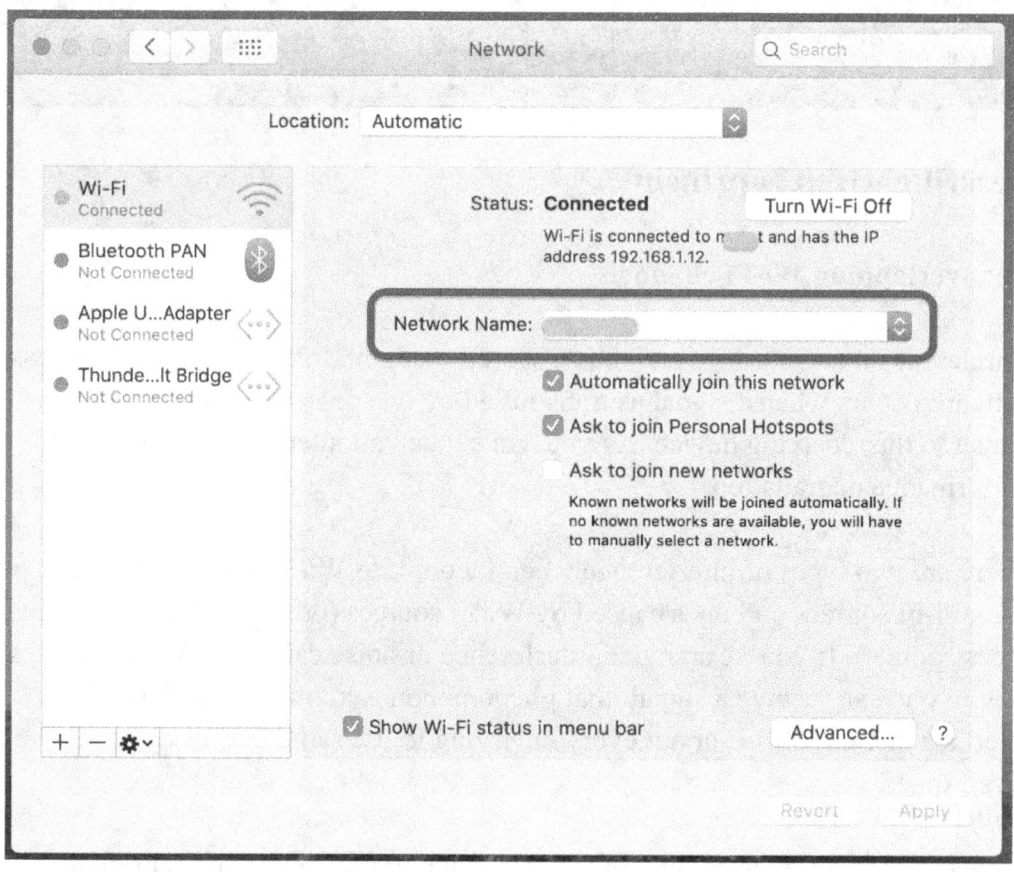

You can also view it using the airport command from within /System/Library/PrivateFrameworks/Apple80211.framework/Versions/Current/Resources.

RF

The power of a radio signal as a function of its ratio to another standard or reference value is measured in decibel (or dB). The two common examples are dBm (dB value is compared to 1mW) and dBw (dB value is compared to 1W).

You can calculate the power in dBs by using the following formula.

Power (dB) = 10 * log10 (Signal / Reference)

Where log10 is logarithm base 10, signal is the power of the signal (in watts), and reference is the reference or standard power (in mW). Below is a list of commonly used dB values for power estimates.

	+3 dB / -3 dB	+10 dB / -10 dB	+30 dB / -30 dB
Increase (+) of	3 dB: Doubles Tx power	10 dB: x10 Tx power	30 dB: x1000 Tx power
Decrease (-) of	3 dB: Halves Tx power	10 dB: 1/10 Tx power	30 dB: x1/1000 Tx power

The radiated or transmitted power is rated in either dBm or W. Power that comes off an antenna is measured as effective isotropic radiated power or EIRP. EIRP is used by regulatory organizations such as the FCC or Europe's ETSI to determine and measure power limits in WLAN equipment.

You can also view Wi-Fi RF parameters by using the macOS Wireless diagnostic tools such as the Info.

```
●●●                    Info
Wi-Fi
  Interface Name         en0
  MAC Address            dc:a9:04:7c:7a:e7
  Power State            On
  Network Name           ████████████
  Active PHY Mode        802.11ac
  Security               WPA2 Personal
  BSSID                  14:91:82:96:1f:81
  Country Code           US
  Quality                Excellent
  RSSI                   -44 dBm
  Noise                  -90 dBm
  Tx Rate                867 Mbps
  Channel                36
  Channel Band           5 GHz
  Channel Width          80 MHz
```

Encryption

Explain virtualization fundamentals (virtual machines)

Virtualization is the foundation technology behind a cloud where compute, storage and networking resources can be dynamically partitioned, provisioned and assigned to applications. Virtualized resources pools of compute and storage can be far more easily allocated on-demand and elastically as opposed to their physical variant, for example, a cloud server versus a bare-metal.

Virtualization is also the process of creating a virtual representation of servers, storage, virtual applications, and networks, using software. The purpose of virtualization is to reduce IT expenses while boosting efficiency, flexibility, and scalability for any business. While virtualization has been around for a long time, it was VMware who pioneered x86 server virtualization.

Different types of virtualizations are as follows:
- Server virtualization
- Storage virtualization
- Network virtualization

- Desktop virtualization

Without virtualization, IT organizations will be forced to deploy a lot more servers to keep pace with today's high storage and processor demands. Each of these servers may be operating only at a fraction of their capacity, thus wasting precious resources.

Enter virtualization. Software, known as a hypervisor, is used to simulate hardware devices' functionality and create a virtual computing environment. Hypervisor allows you to split one system into separate virtual environments known as virtual machines (VMs). Hypervisor is simply a layer between the guest VMs and the underlying physical server hardware. Virtual Machines rely on the ability of the hypervisor to separate the machine's resources and distribute them as per the requirement.

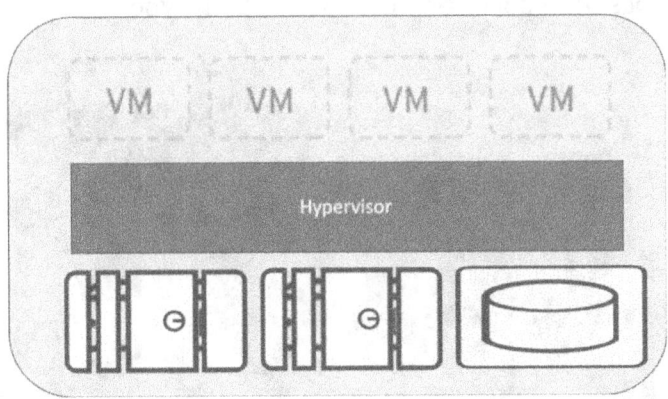

This enables IT organizations to run multiple applications across different operating systems, on a single server. This results in economies of scale and better efficiency.

Some of the additional benefits of virtualization are the following:

- Minimize or reduce downtime.
- Reduced capital and operating costs.
- Increased IT productivity, agility, efficiency and responsiveness.

- Faster provisioning of resources and applications.
- Greater business continuity and disaster recovery.
- Ease of data center management using Software.

Disadvantages of virtualization are the following:

- Increased upfront costs (investing in virtualization software).
- Need to license software.
- There may be a learning curve if IT managers are not experienced.
- Not every application and server will work in a virtualized environment.
- Availability can be an issue if an organization can't connect to their virtualized data.

Hypervisor Type 1 and Type 2

There are two types of hypervisors, i.e. Type-1 and Type-2.

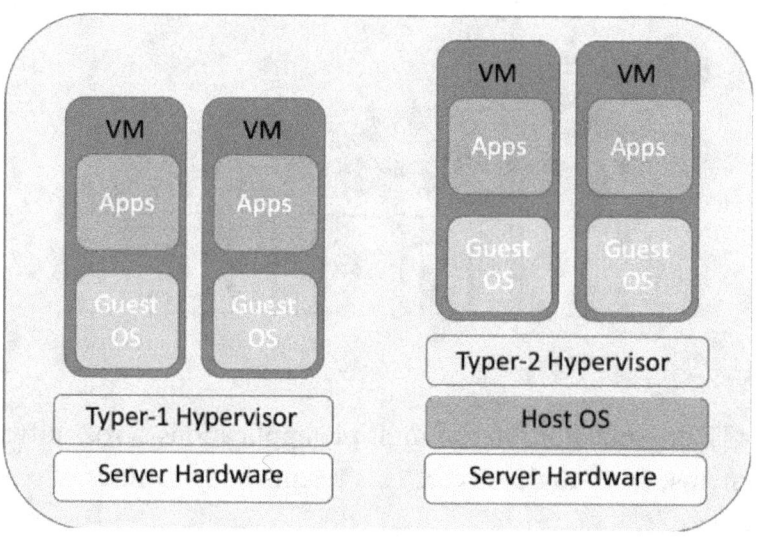

Type-1 hypervisor runs on the physical hardware of the host machine. It doesn't have to load an underlying operating system first. With direct access to the underlying hardware and no other software, these hypervisors are the most efficient hypervisors by running directly atop bare metal.

A Type-2 hypervisor is typically installed on top of an existing operating system and known as a hosted hypervisor. Type-2 hypervisors are generally not used for data center computing and are reserved for client or end-user, where performance and security are of lesser concern.

Before we move on, it is worth noting that terms hypervisor and Virtual Machine Monitor (or VMM) are often used interchangeably, but, they do not exactly refer to the same piece of software. Hypervisor (or more precisely Type-1 hypervisor) includes VMM as well as the device model. You can think of VMM as software responsible for setting up VMs and handling I/O access for guest OS. VMM ensures that guest OS execution has pretty much identical behavior while running on top of VMM versus bare metal. It is also responsible for efficient program execution as well as managing all hardware resources. The device model is the other part of the hypervisor which provides I/O interfaces for VMs by way of I/O virtualization. VMM delegates I/O requests to the correct device model. You can think of vNICs and vHBAs as examples of various device models. Device model can be either software-based (e.g. virtIO drivers) or hardware-based or hardware-assisted (e.g. SR-IOV which allows a physical PCIe function to be partitioned into multiple virtual PCIe functions). With software-based solutions, I/O virtualization techniques simply use virtualized CPUs (or vCPUs) alongside the VMs.

Virtual Machine

The virtual machine (or VM) is comprised of a set of configuration and specification files. It comes to life using the physical resources of the underlying host. Each VM is self-contained and is completely independent of other VMs. Multiple VMs can be installed on the same physical server, which enables several operating systems and applications to run on one physical server or host. A thin layer of hypervisor software decouples the virtual machines from the host. It also takes care of dynamically allocating the required resources to each virtual machine.

A virtual machine consists of several types of files that are stored on the supported storage device. The key files that are part of any virtual machine are the virtual disk file, NVRAM setting file, configuration file, and the log file. You can configure a virtual machine using the given virtualization software. You do not need to edit any of the key files, manually.

A virtual machine may contain extra files, if you add Raw Device Mappings (RDMs) or if one or more snapshots exist.

Every virtual machine has virtual devices that provide the same functionality as physical devices. It has additional benefits in terms of portability, manageability, and security.

Key Properties of Virtual Machines are as follows

- Encapsulation
- Hardware Independence
- Isolation
- Partitioning

Compute virtualization is a simplification of legacy architecture to reduce the total number of physical servers. Server virtualization allows us to run multiple operating systems on a single physical machine, where each OS can run inside a separate virtual machine or VM. x86 server virtualization was pioneered by VMware in the late 1990s.

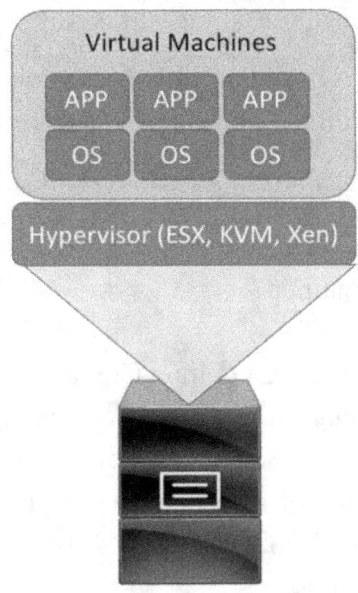

Physical Server

There are numerous benefits of compute virtualization including but not limited to the following.
- Improved security
- Easier administration
- Cost savings
- Consolidation and centralization of physical servers
- Faster TTM

Containers

A container image is a lightweight, portable and executable package of software that consists of code, runtime libraries, system tools, and libraries, etc. Containers are available for both Linux and Windows-based apps.

There are a variety of container technologies that exist today.

- Docker containers

- Java containers
- Unikernels
- LXD (LXD is based on liblxc, its purpose is to control some lxc with added capabilities, like snapshots or live migration)
- OpenVZ
- Rkt
- Windows server containers
- Hyper-V container

It is worth noting that LXCs (Linux Containers) are an OS-level virtualization mechanism for running multiple isolated Linux systems (or containers) on a control host using a single Linux kernel. LXD isn't a repackaging of LXC, in fact, it was built on top of LXC to provide a new, better user experience. Technically speaking, LXD uses LXC through liblxc and its Go binding to create and manage the containers.

Docker Containers

The most popular way to containerize an application is to deploy it as a docker container. Docker is an open platform for developers and sysadmins to build, ship, and run distributed applications, whether on laptops, data center VMs, or the cloud. Docker can build images automatically by reading the instructions from a Dockerfile. A Dockerfile is a text file that contains all the commands a user could call on the command line to assemble an image. In Docker, everything is based on Images. An image is a combination of a file system and parameters. A container is a runtime instance of an image. It lays out the steps the "docker build' command needs to take in order to create an image that can be used to create the actual container.

You can get a list of Docker images on your local by using "docker images" command. By default, docker related files are located under /var/lib/docker folder. It is a simple text file, named Dockerfile.

```
netdevops@netdevops-VirtualBox:/var/lib/docker$ sudo ls
builder      containers   network      plugins      swarm        trust
containerd   image                     overlay2     runtimes     tmp          volumes
```

Container image contains executable package of a piece of software that includes everything needed to run it: code, runtime, system tools, system libraries, settings.

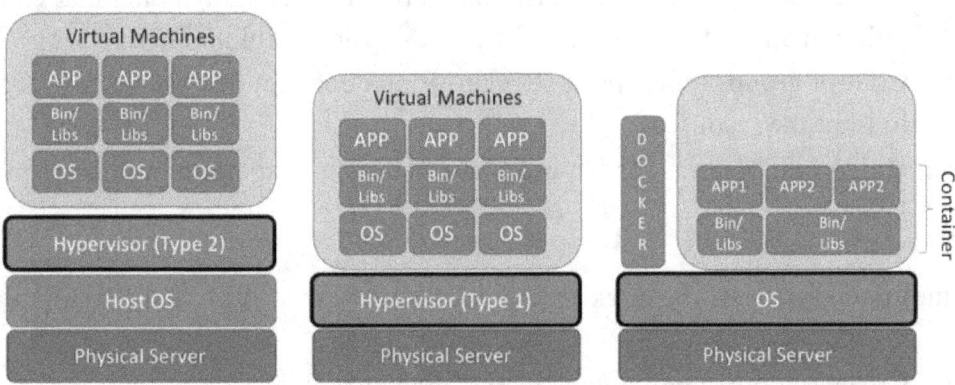

It is crucial to understand the difference between a VM and a container. Containers are an abstraction at the app layer that packages code and dependencies together whereas VMs are an abstraction of physical hardware, turning one server into many virtual ones.

	Virtual Machine (VM)	Docker Container
Host OS	Yes	N/A
Hypervisor	Yes	N/A
Guest OS	Yes	N/A
Bins/Libraries	Yes	Yes
Application	Yes	Yes

Typical Size (bytes)	Tens of GBs	Tens of MBs
Startup time	Slower	Faster

There are three fundamental technologies, when put together, provide us the overall container technology.

- Namespaces (helps isolate different parts of the running container, e.g. pid, mnt and net namespaces for process, filesystem and networking)
- Control groups (cgroups, a standard Linux concept that allows a system to limit the resources)
- Union File systems (or UnionFS are file systems that are built layer by layer)

A simplified version of the docker container workflow looks like the following.

- Create or copy a new image using "docker build"
- Run a container ("docker run" or "docker container create")
- The docker daemon checks if it has a local copy of the image, else pulls the image from registry
- The docker daemon creates a container based on the image. If "docker run" command was used, it will log into it and execute the requested command.

Here is a list of commands that can be used inside a Dockerfile.

- FROM
- MAINTAINER
- RUN
- CMD
- EXPOSE
- ENV
- COPY

- ENTRYPOINT
- VOLUME
- USER
- WORKDIR
- ARG
- ONBUILD
- STOPSIGNAL
- LABEL

You can start a docker container locally by using the following command. The "-d" parameter is short for --detach and means that we want to run it in the background whereas the "-P" tells Docker to publish it on the ports that we exposed.

```
sudo docker run -d -P my-app-image
```

You can see your container by listing the Linux processes.

```
sudo docker ps
```

If you want to make your Docker images available to others, you need to store it in an image registry. By default, Docker uses the Docker Hub registry however you can also create and use your own. A registry stores a collection of repositories, i.e. where you store one or more versions of a specific Docker image. You can publish your image into repo but first committing your container "sudo docker commit" and then push the image to the repo using "sudo docker push" command. You can't help but notice that this process looks like how version control systems such as Git work.

Describe switching concepts

MAC learning and aging

Ternary Content Addressable Memory (or TCAM) is a type of CAM that can operate with 0, 1 and X where X refers to either a 0 or 1 hence giving it more flexibility in terms of searching through memory locations within CAM. When a frame is received on a switch port with TCAM, a copy of the first 200 bytes of the packet is copied to the forwarding controller which helps perform the actual lookups within the TCAM. Those 200 bytes are enough to perform all necessary forwarding decisions based on VLANs, egress ports, etc.

Each TCAM entry comprises three components, i.e. Value, Mask and Result. The X value that I referred to earlier is organized by the mask where each unique mask can represent up to eight values. The mask/value pairs are evaluated simultaneously in order to find the best or the longest match within a single TCAM lookup operation. In the case of an ACL, once a source/destination mask pair reaches eight values, a new mask pair is created so another eight values can be stored.

TCAM is carved into five main working areas, i.e.

- Layer 2
- Layer 3
- QoS Access Control Elements (or individual permit/deny statements)
- Security Access Control Elements (or individual permit/deny statements)
- IPv6

There are some notable differences between high-end and low-end switching platforms when it comes to their use and size of TCAMs. For example, higher-end switches come with larger TCAM sizes and do not make use of Switching Database Manager (or SDM) templates.

Frame switching

Frame switching is the process as to how two end hosts communicate with each other on an ethernet segment. Much like network layer and IP addresses, the data link layer also has its link-layer addresses which are known as MAC addresses for ethernet. If you two end hosts are on the same IP subnet, they do not need a default gateway or a router to communicate with each other. One end-host can use ARP to find out the other's MAC address on an ethernet segment, and then simply transmit the packet to the destination host. However, when the destination host is on a different subnet than the source host, the source host would simply send that packet off to the default gateway or the router. If the router knows how to reach that destination IP subnet, via a static or dynamic routing protocol, the router will simply rewrite the L2 information and send packet off to its destination host using the appropriate outgoing interface.

In the earliest days of networking, Cisco routers switched packets from incoming to outgoing interfaces using process switching which was slow due to the CPU overhead involved. Eventually, Cisco streamlined the process with fast switching and then finally CEF switching

Frame flooding

Ethernet switches forward frames based on their MAC tables which is built using the frames' source MAC addresses and the corresponding ports they were received on during the Learning stage. Every time switch receives a new frame, it looks up the destination MAC address in the MAC table for a possible match, if there is a match, it forwards the frame to that port.

But what if the switch doesn't have a matching entry, then it simply floods the frame to all switch ports except the one it was received on. Switch also performs flooding when the incoming frame has a broadcast (FF:FF:FF:FF:FF:FF), common with ARP and DHCP protocols, as the destination MAC address. Flooding is when a switch acts like a hub.

MAC address table

MAC address table is what's also known as the CAM table and is used on switches to find the egress port for frame forwarding. MAC address table timeout is five minutes by default on Cisco switches, so entry is held in the table only for that amount of time before the timeout expires and the entry is removed from the table.

Switch#show mac address-table

```
          Mac Address Table
-------------------------------------------
Vlan    Mac Address      Type       Ports
----    -----------     --------   -----
  1     00ld.70ab.5d80   DYNAMIC    Fa0/3
  1     00le.f724.al80   DYNAMIC    Fa0/4
```

Total Mac Addresses for this criterion: 2

Chapter Summary

- Routers route traffic across IP subnets based on the destination IP address or prefix.
- L2 Switches are for bridging or forwarding traffic based on the destination MAC address within a given L2 segment
- In Cisco's Unified Wireless Network architecture, access points are known as Lightweight APs (LAPs). The other types of APs are standalone and do not require WLCs.
- Two-layer DC design is a modified three-layer design where the core has been collapsed into the distribution layer.
- Wide Area Network (WAN) is a network connectivity medium that spans a large geographical area
- Single mode (SMF) means the fiber enables one type of light mode to be propagated at a time, whereas multimode (MMF) means that the fiber can propagate multiple modes.
- Power over Ethernet (PoE) describes a mechanism where power is passed along with data on a twister pair ethernet cabling
- Collision occurs when two or more stations try to transmit at the same time
- This is a frame that is shorter than 64 bytes.
- An IP subnet is an isolated IP or L3 segment
- Private IP networks, as opposed to their public counterpart, are not allocated to any specific organization.
- IPv6 address space expands the number of address bits from 32-bit (in IPv4) to 128-bit
- A unique local address (ULA) is like an RFC 1918 private IPv4 address
- Adjacent channel interference (or ACI) is when transmissions are sent on an adjacent or partially overlapping channel. ACI occurs as a result of bleed over to an overlapping channel which causes noise and interference.
- The power of a radio signal as a function of its ratio to another standard or reference value is measured in decibel (or dB).
- Type-1 hypervisor runs on the physical hardware of the host machine

- MAC address table is what's also known as the CAM table and is used on switches to find the egress port for frame forwarding

CHAPTER 2 NETWORK ACCESS

This chapter covers the following exam topics from Cisco's official 200-901 V1.0[8] Network Associate (CCNA) exam blueprint.

- Configure and verify VLANs (normal range) spanning multiple switches
    - Access ports (data and voice)
    - Default VLAN
    - Connectivity
- Configure and verify interswitch connectivity
    - Trunk ports
    - 802.1Q
    - Native VLAN
- Configure and verify Layer 2 discovery protocols (Cisco Discovery Protocol and LLDP)
- Configure and verify (Layer 2/Layer 3) EtherChannel (LACP)
- Describe the need for and basic operations of Rapid PVST+ Spanning Tree Protocol and identify basic operations
    - Root port, root bridge (primary/secondary), and other port names
    - Port states (forwarding/blocking)
    - PortFast benefits
- Compare Cisco Wireless Architectures and AP modes
- Describe physical infrastructure connections of WLAN components (AP, WLC, access/trunk ports, and LAG)
- Describe AP and WLC management access connections (Telnet, SSH, HTTP, HTTPS, console, and TACACS+/RADIUS)
- Configure the components of a wireless LAN access for client connectivity using GUI only such as WLAN creation, security settings, QoS profiles, and advanced WLAN settings

---

[8] https://bit.ly/2PGgv4A

Configure and verify VLANs (normal range) spanning multiple switches

Virtual LAN (or VLAN) is a broadcast domain that is partitioned virtually to carve out an isolated L2 segment. VLANs are identified by VLAN IDs which is a 12-bit VID field inside the IEEE 802.1Q header. 12-bit allows for ID allocation from 0 to 4095 ($2^{12} - 1$).

Access ports (data and voice)

An access port is a port on a switch that is used to transmit data to and from a specific access VLAN connected to an endpoint such as a bare metal server or a VM. Access port, as opposed to the trunk port, does not accept tagged traffic. If an access port accidentally receives traffic from another VLAN (tagged with another VLAN), it simply drops the packets without learning its MAC source address.

Default and Native VLANs

Any traffic coming on a switch trunk port (ethernet port connecting a switch to another) that is not tagged with a VLAN ID, will be assigned a native VLAN tag which is VLAN ID 1 for Cisco switches. As opposed to trunk ports, access ports expect all traffic to receive untagged and will send traffic forward (or upstream) tagged with the pre-configured VLAN ID, a default ID (also ID 1 for Cisco) will be used if none configured by the administrator. In conclusion, both native and default VLAN IDs are set to 1 on Cisco devices, however, they exist in two different scenarios i.e. trunk versus access ports.

Connectivity

While all devices within a VLAN are L2 adjacent so they can communicate simply based on ARP resolution (IP to MAC). However, inter-VLAN communication requires routing which is done by an L3 switch or a router.

During VLAN creation process, you can set the following parameters.

- VLAN number
- VLAN name
- VLAN type
- VLAN state
- MTU

L2 Switches are for bridging or forwarding traffic based on the destination MAC address within a given L2 segment or VLAN based on CAM table which is built using the source MAC addresses. L3 switches can function both as an L2 switch as well as a router for inter-VLAN routing and many other use cases. Nexus series products represent Cisco's family of switches.

The following steps describe the switching process.

- The switch receives a frame from a source machine
- The switch stores the source MAC address and the switch port that the frame was received on into the MAC table.
- The switch checks the table for the matching destination MAC address. If there is a match, that port is used to forward the frame. If there is no match, it is flooded out of all the switch ports (for that VLAN).

Configure and verify interswitch connectivity

Trunk ports

The trunk is an L2 feature that uses 802.1Q VLAN tags to multiplex (or trunk) traffic from multiple VLANs on a single physical link. The Trunk can be configured either manually by the network admin, or a protocol such as DTP or VTP can be used to facilitate the propagation of VLAN configuration within a switching domain.

802.1Q

IEEE 802.1Q, also referred to as dot1q, is an ethernet standard that supports VLANs. It defines a system where traffic from individual VLANs is identified using a 2-byte tag. Tagging is the mechanism by which you can aggregate traffic to and from multiple VLANs onto single port.

DA	SA	Tag	Type/Length	Data	FCS	
6	6	4	2	Up to 1500	4	bytes

Tag Control Information (TCI)

TPID	Priority	CFI	VID	
16	3	1	12	bits
Tag Protocol Identifier (Typically 0x8100 (default), 0x9100 or 0x9200)	802.1 p priority levels (0 to 7)	Canonical Format Indicator 0 = canonical MAC 1 = non - canonical MAC	Unique VLAN identifier (0 to 4095)	

IEEE 802.3ac Ethernet VLAN Tag

Native VLAN

A trunk port can carry 802.1Q tagged traffic from various VLANs as well as untagged traffic. The native VLAN ID is the VLAN that carries untagged traffic on the trunk ports. The native VLAN ID # must match on both ends of the trunk port. If you do not configure a native VLAN ID, a Cisco switch will use the default VLAN (VLAN 1) as the native VLAN ID.

Configure and verify Layer 2 discovery protocols (Cisco Discovery Protocol and LLDP)

Cisco Discovery Protocol (CDP) is a Cisco proprietary (closed source) data link layer protocol. It is used to share information about other directly connected

Cisco or equipment from other vendors that support CDP. The information that can be communicated using CDP includes the operating system version and IP addresses. All CDP packets include a VLAN ID. If you configure CDP on a Layer 2 access port, the CDP packets sent from that access port include the VLAN ID configured on the access port. If you configure CDP on a Layer 2 trunk port, the CDP packets sent from that trunk port include the lowest configured VLAN ID allowed on that trunk port.

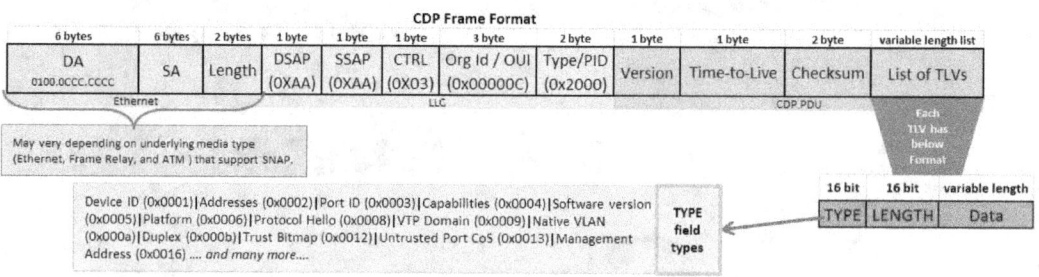

Link Layer Discovery Protocol (LLDP) is a vendor-neutral link layer protocol developed by IEEE. It is used by networking devices such as routers and switches for advertising their identity, capabilities, and neighbors on a LAN. The topology of an LLDP-enabled network can be discovered by *crawling* the hosts and querying this database. There are three mandatory TLVs that are used during the discovery process namely chassis ID, port ID and TTL.

Both CDP and LLDP are enabled by default. If you prefer not to use the CDP or LDDP capabilities, you can disable them by using the following commands.

	CDP commands	**LLDP commands**
Enable Globally	cdp run	lldp run
Enable Locally (Interface)	cdp enable	lldp transmit lldp receive
Disable Globally	no cdp run	no lldp run
Disable Locally (Interface)	no cdp enable	no lldp transmit no lldp receive

You can verify whether CDP or LLDP is enabled or disabled on your Cisco device using the following commands.

	CDP commands	**LLDP commands**
Verification	show cdp neighbors show cdp show cdp interface show cdp traffic	show lldp show lldp configuration show lldp interface

Configure and verify (Layer 2/Layer 3) EtherChannel (LACP)

EthernetChannel allows bonding or bundling of up to 8 ethernet links into one logical link. If one link within the bundle were to fail, the switch will automatically move traffic to other functional links. As far as STP is concerned, it sees EtherChannel as one logical link thus avoiding any potential conflict with respect to bridging loops. EtherChannels are also known as Port Channels.

EtherChannels are not be confused with trunks since trunks are used to allow traffic from more than one VLAN on a given port (trunk), whereas EtherChannels are simply a bundle of two or more ports that provide higher bandwidth, load balancing, and link-level redundancy. Unlike trunks, EtherChannels can be configured as L2 as well as L3 links.

EtherChannel can be configured manually (aka statically) by the network admin, or a dynamic protocol can be used to perform link negotiation. There are two common types of protocols, i.e. Port Aggregation Protocol (or Cisco proprietary

PAgP) and Link Aggregation Control Protocol (or IEEE 802.3ad LACP). For all practical purposes, you will always be configuring LACP.

For EthernetChannel troubleshooting, you can always use show etherchannel summary command as a starting point to prod EtherChannel status. You can verify the channel negotiation mode by using show etherchannel port command.

For etherchannel to work, each side must have the same switch mode, i.e. access or trunk, native and trunked VLAN, port speed and duplex, etc.

Describe the need for and basic operations of Rapid PVST+ Spanning Tree

Protocol and identify basic operations

Rapid PVST+ is an improved implementation of the original STP that allows you to create one STP topology for each VLAN. Rapid PVST+ is the default STP mode on Cisco switches.

Let's assume Switch A is connected to Switch B through a p2p link and all the ports are in the blocking state.

- Switch A sends a proposal message to switch B, proposing itself as the designated switch
- Switch B selects as its new root por the port from which the proposal message was received. It then sends out an agreement message back to switch A.
- After receiving the agreement message from switch B, switch A also immediately transitions its designated port to the forwarding state. All non-edge ports on switch B are blocked because there is a p2p link between switch A and B.
- When switch C connects to switch B, it goes through the similar handshaking mechanism. Switch C selects the port connected to switch B as its root port and ports on both ends transition to forwarding state.

- As the network continues to converge, the same handshaking mechanism progresses from the root towards the leaves of the spanning tree.

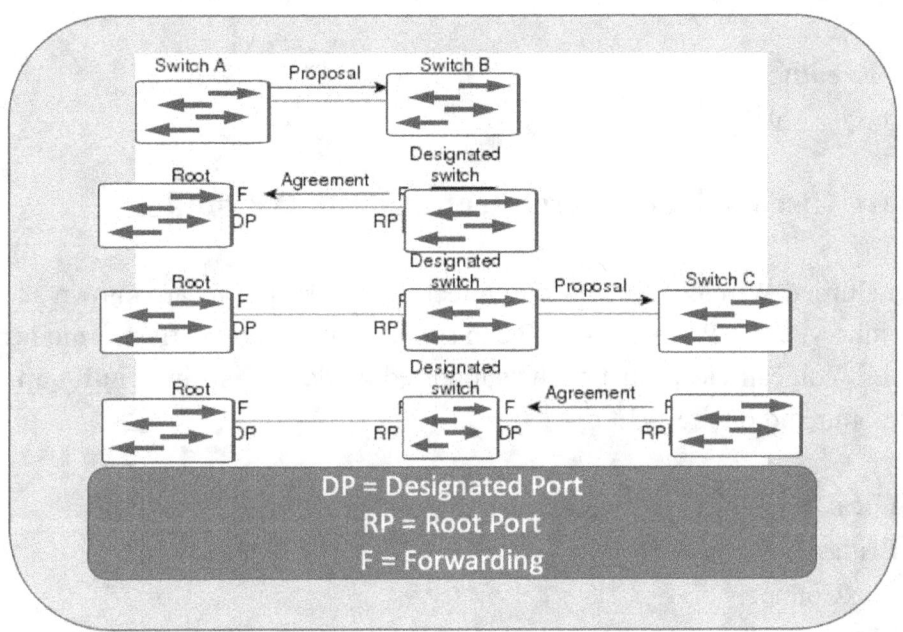

Root port, root bridge (primary/secondary), and other port names

Root port is a forwarding port that is the best port from a non-root switch or bridge to a root switch. A designated port is a forwarding port for every LAN segment. The edge ports are the ports that are directed connected to end stations.

Port states (forwarding/blocking)

A port in the forwarding state forwards frames across the network segment and processes BPDUs. It is the normal state in the STP finite state machine.

A port in blocking state doesn't forward frames received on the port.

PortFast benefits

PortFast is a Cisco proprietary feature that can help edge ports transition to forwarding states quickly. A cisco switch does not generate Topology Change Notification (TCN) BPDU for the ports with port fast feature enabled.

Further Reading
https://bit.ly/2ASHKVG

Compare Cisco Wireless Architectures and AP modes

In Cisco Unified Wireless Network architecture, access points are known as Lightweight APs (LAPs). Cisco LAP can support up to eight different modes of operations. You can view a list of the supported modes by issuing **config ap mode ?** command on the WLC.

- Local
- Bridge
- FlexConnect
- Monitor
- Reap
- Rogue
- SE-Connect
- Sniffer

The most common and well-known AP mode is known as Local. It is also the default mode of operation. In local mode, LAP maintains a CAPWAP tunnel to its associated controller. All client traffic is centrally forwarded by the controller, the reason why LAPs are known as dumb APs. Without connection to a controller, LAP will not forward any traffic.

Remote Edge Lightweight Access Point or REAP, Hybrid-Reap (H-Reap) or FlexConnect always addresses the scalability issue with Local mode by not mandating connectivity to a controller. FlexConnect is just another name for H-Reap.

Monitor mode is a feature designed to allow LWAPP-enabled APs to exclude themselves from dealing with data traffic between clients and the infrastructure. In this mode, LAPs act as dedicated sensors for location-based services or LBS. In this mode, APs cannot serve clients.

Bridge mode is used for bridging the wireless and wired infrastructure together. It is one of the oldest modes around.

SE-Connect mode allows you to connect to LAP using the Cisco Spectrum Expert to gather statistics. It is used for troubleshooting purposes only.

Sniffer is also like SE-Connect mode and is used for troubleshooting purposes only.
Rouge Detector is yet again like SE-Connect and Sniffer modes, it doesn't serve any clients and is used for security purposes against rogue APs.

Centralized (Local-Mode) Model

This model is primarily recommended for large site deployments. There are multiple benefits to centralized deployments.

- Easier IP address management
- Simplified configuration and troubleshooting
- Roaming at scale

You can connect the WLAN controller in a variety of ways, i.e. directly to a DC services module or block, a separate services block within the campus core or distribution layer in your 3-tier design. Wireless traffic is usually tunneled via the Control and Provisioning of Wireless Access Points (CAPWAP) protocol which operates between the WLAN controller and the AP.

Thanks to its centralized nature, policy application is straightforward in this model because the controller is your single point for managing L2 security and network policies thus providing a unifying policy application across wireless and wired.

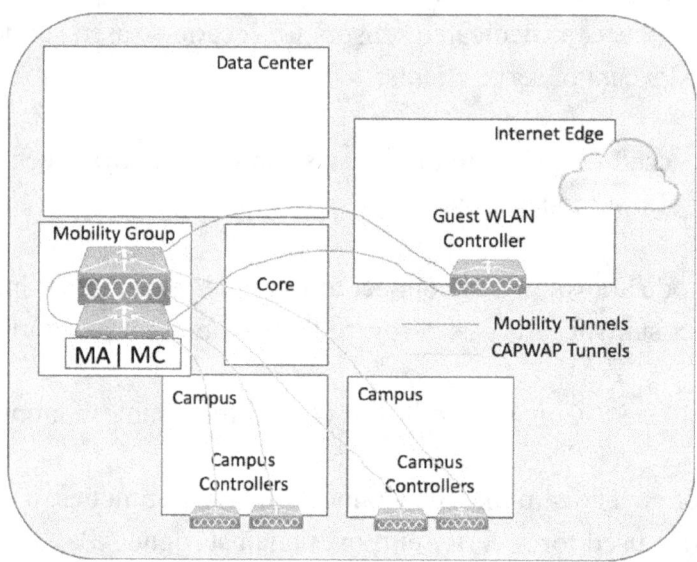

In terms of direct customer benefits, local-mode provides the delivery on the following requirements.

- It enables fast roaming so wireless users can roam all they want between floors and buildings all over the campus.
- It can support rich media services with Call Admission Control (CAC) and multicast with Cisco VideoStream.
- It allows for centralized policy enforcement where you can subject your traffic to the firewall (L4-L7 inspection), network access control and classification.

For larger centralized or local-mode deployments, it is recommended that you use the Cisco 8540 or 5520 WLAN controllers. For smaller sites, Cisco recommends that you use a 3504 WLAN controller as a local on-site controller.

In this model, APs are referred to as thin APs.

Distributed Model

The distributed WLAN architecture or design is where wireless traffic load is distributed across various access points, so it is the opposite of centralized or local-mode design as far as traffic handling is concerned. In this mode, you must reconfigure your access layer every time you add an AP. This model uses distributed forwarding as the forwarding of data between the client and destination happens directly through the AP without the intermediary step of being tunneled through a controller as is the case with a centralized approach. In this model, APs are referred to as fat APs.

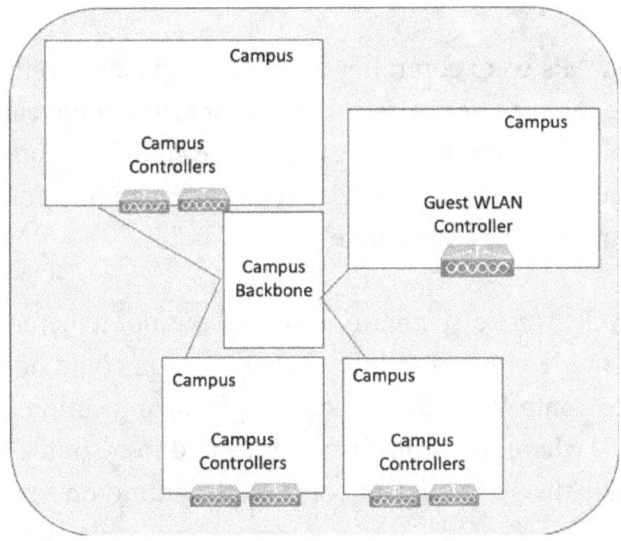

Distributed WLCs are commonly connected to the distribution layer within the campus network, and in that case, Cisco doesn't recommend using an L2 to hook up a WLC as that would require adding access layer features such as HSRP to the distribution layer. Cisco strongly recommends using WLC via L3 which allows for WLAN configuration to be isolated on a single device much like other access layer routing devices.

Controller-less Model

The controller-less deployment still uses controller functionality but in a virtual or hosted fashion. With the rise of controller-less APs, you don't need a physical controller to drive a bunch of APs, so you simply move that controller function i.e. control and management planes to another entity on or off-site.

Controller-based Model

It is worth recapping a little bit of WLAN history here. Remember, WLAN started with standalone APs with no centralized coordination of any sort whatsoever, so those APs were independent in every way you can imagine. You would need to log into each of them and hand configure pretty much.

Second generation APs were controller-based, or you can also them dependent or tethered i.e. they couldn't operate on their own or without the centralized controller. WLAN controller used to be expensive so unless you can throw more controllers to achieve your desired HA, you pretty much had no choice but to deal with the controller being the single point of failure.

Third generation APs were also controller-based but not tethered but tunneled which solved the single point of failure issue since you could now build a tunnel all the way back to controller regardless of its physical location. This also created a drawback where the controller still needed to be in the forwarding path. You still needed expensive redundant controllers and it didn't scale well in larger deployments.

This brings us to the fourth generation, i.e. cloud-based approach.

Cloud-based Model

Cloud-based architecture offers significant advantages over legacy hardware-based controller devices so, in your actual WLAN deployment, you only focus on the APs. All your configuration, optimization, and mobility control are centralized and delivered to you as a cloud service from the providers hosted data center.

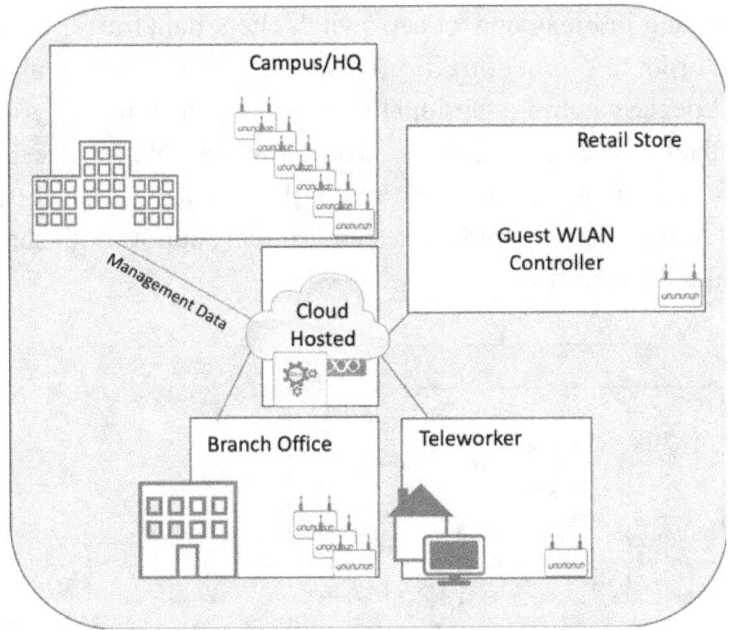

This model provides significant benefits over legacy approaches primarily due to less hardware to buy, install and maintain.

- Speed and ease of deployment
- Cost savings
- Better HA
- Better performance (no data tunneling to cloud-based controller)
- Simplified multi-site and remote site setup
- Effortless upgrades

Remote Branch Model

Cisco FlexConnect is the go-to model for multiple small remote sites or branches that connect into a central site. FlexConnect provides a cost-effective solution where network engineers can control remote APs from headquarters through the WAN.

Cisco AP operating in FlexConnect can switch client data traffic with dot1q VLAN tags in order to segment traffic. This mode of operation is also known as FlexConnect Local Switching. Optionally, in FlexConnect mode, you can also tunnel traffic back to the centralized controller for example for guest access. FlexConnect can be deployed in either a shared or dedicated controller model. Cisco WLAN 8500, 550 and 3500 series controllers support both shared and dedicated modes of operation.

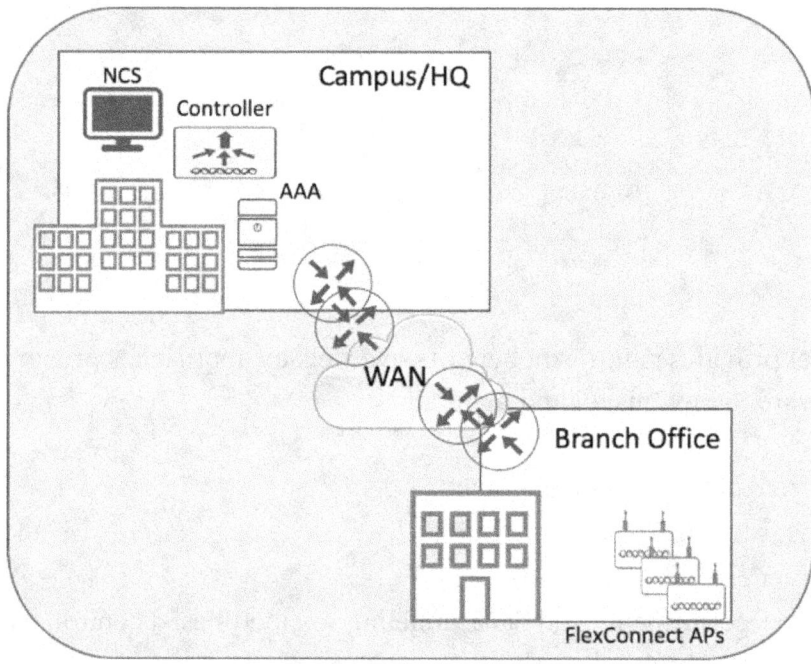

Before you use shared mode, make sure that your deployments meet the following requirements.

- You have an existing local-mode controller pair on the HQ
- Controller pair has adequate capacity to support Cisco FlexConnect APs
- Your controller pair meets or exceeds the FlexConnect group's requirements

For HA purposes, you can deploy a pair of controllers in SSO configuration or N+1 arrangement if you desire cross-site resiliency. Alternatively, you can also deploy dual resilient controllers configured in an N+1 manner using the Cisco vWLC.

SD-Access Wireless Model

SD-Access Wireless is the fabric-enabled wireless solution that also fully integrates with a wired SD-Access design. The primary benefit of SD-Access Wireless is that customers can have a unified policy and experience across both wired and wireless mediums. In this design, the fabric WLCs communicate wireless client information to the fabric control plane, and the fabric APs encapsulate traffic into the VXLAN data path.

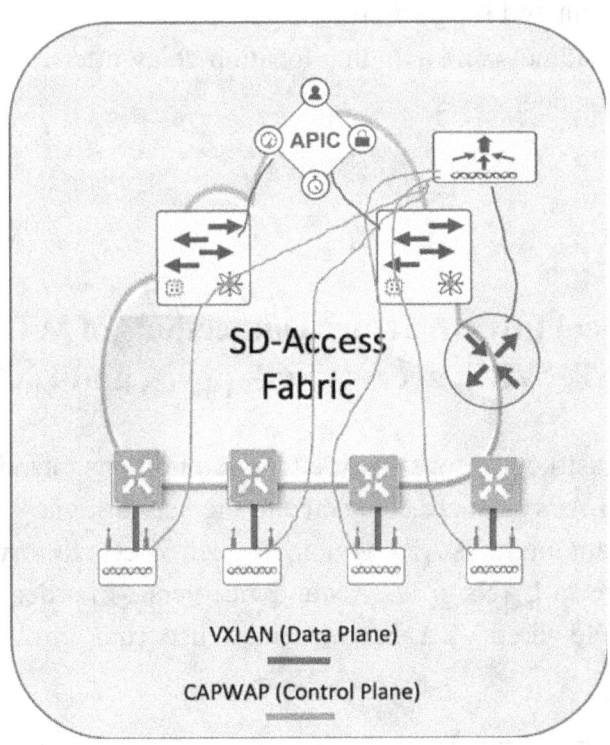

Location services in a WLAN design

In the early days of WLAN deployments, focus used to be mostly around providing maximum Wi-Fi coverage with the minimum AP count possible, fast forward to today, coverage uniformity and cell to cell overlap are now the major areas of design consideration. This change has been mostly driven by applications such as voice or video which have a lower tolerance to jitter and roaming delays.

Cisco's best practices in designing and deploying location-aware WLANs include the following components.

- Minimal signal level thresholds
- AP placement and separation
- Location readiness and avoiding location delay jitter
- Antenna considerations

Further Reading
Cisco Campus LAN and WLAN Design Guide[9]

Describe physical infrastructure connections of WLAN components (AP, WLC, access/trunk ports, and LAG)

Cisco WLAN infrastructure consists of either autonomous (standalone) or lightweight APs (LAPs) that are connected to the network via WLAN controllers. With autonomous APs, you don't need WLCs to forward ethernet frames from a wired VLANs to WLAN and vice versa. In order to aggregate traffic from multiple wired VLANs, you need to use trunk links as shown in the diagram below.

---

[9] https://bit.ly/31lkl2O

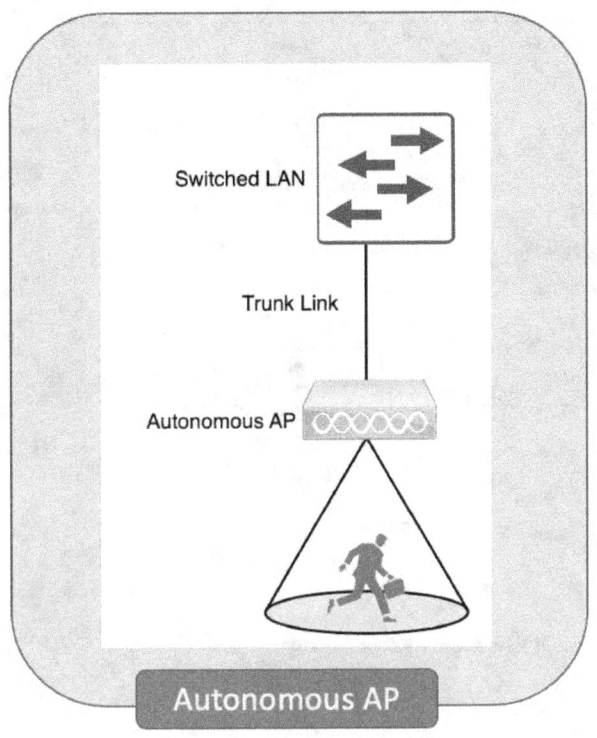

The autonomous AP maps each VLAN to a WLAN and BSS and maintains a single physical connection via the trunk interface. You must configure the switch port as trunk port using the Dot1q tagging so each frame is tagged with the VLAN ID it came from. The wireless side of the AP marks packets from each VLAN with the corresponding BSSID of the WLAN.

The LAP also has a single wired ethernet interface, but it is paired with a WLC which helps map and tunnel traffic from several wired VLANs with the help of CAPWAP protocol. As a result, each LAP is connected to the switch via an access port. The CAPWAP tunnel is used for tunneling traffic from VLANs as shown in the figure below.

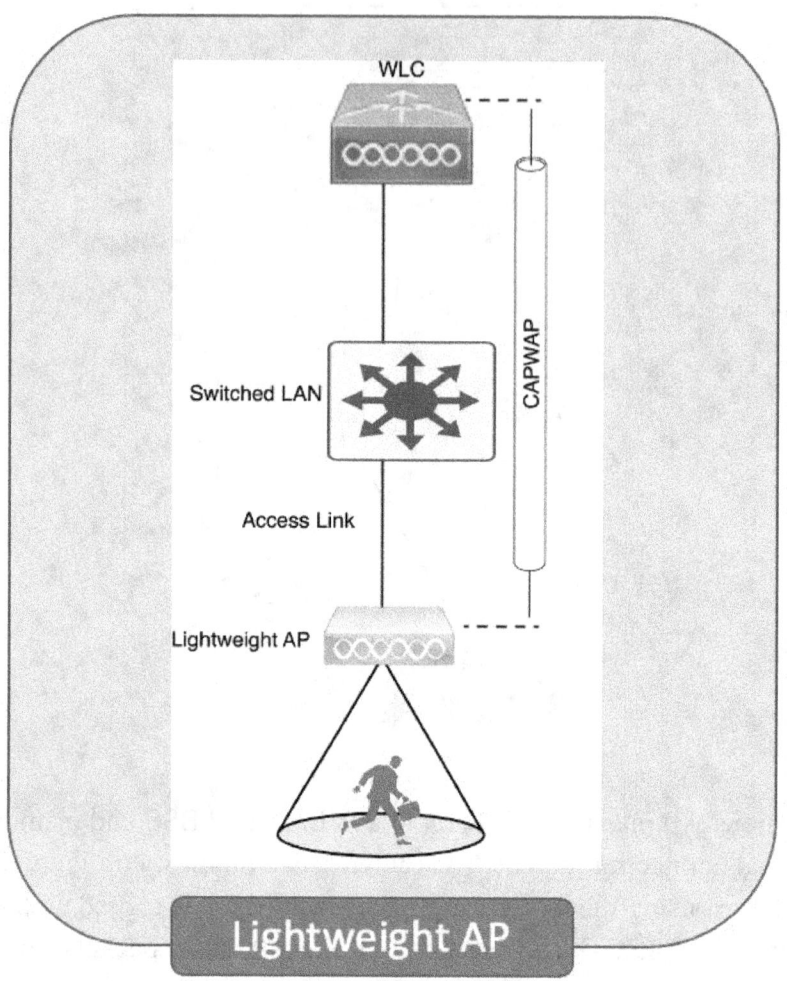

You can connect several types of controller interfaces or ports to your switch.

- Service port: It is used for out of band management.
- Distribution system port: It is used for all AP and WLC management traffic.
- Console port: It is used for out of band management.
- Redundancy port: It is used to connect to another WLC for HA.

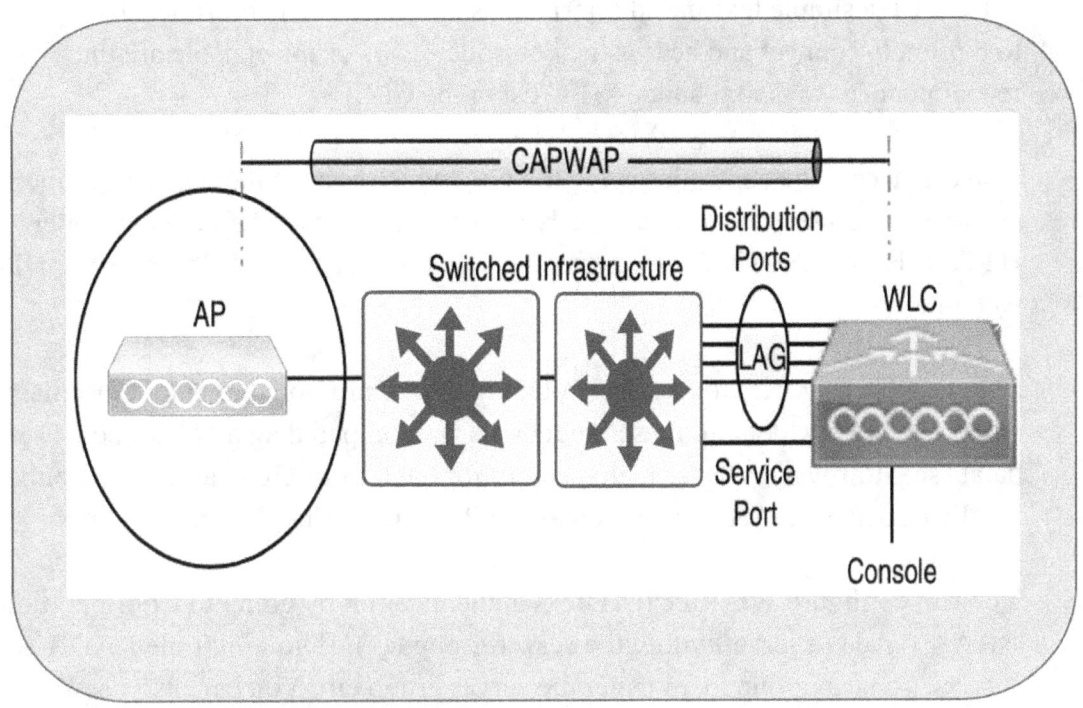

To get the most out of each distribution system port, you can configure all of them as an EtherChannel or a link aggregation group (LAG). LAG provides traffic load balancing and resilience against port level failure. You need to configure the LAG port on the switch side as always-on since WLCs do not support EtherChannel or LAG.

Describe AP and WLC management access connections (Telnet, SSH, HTTP, HTTPS, console, and TACACS+/RADIUS)

A Cisco WLC can be managed using a either the CLI or the GUI. You can use variety of protocols such as the telnet/SSH or console port to access WLC using the CLI. You can also use HTTP/HTTPS protocol to access WLC using the GUI.

WLC CLI, a simple text-based interface, is built into each controller. It allows up to 5 users to connect and access the controller. SSH or the console are the recommended ways to manage WLC using the CLI.

You can access the controller using the GUI which is built into each controller. It allows up to 5 users to simultaneously connect and browse into the controller. HTTPS (HTTP/SSL) is the recommended way to manage WLC using the GUI or web interface.

Every time a user tries to access a WLC, it will be prompted to enter a username and password. By default, these credentials are compared against the local user database. However, the user management for the CLI or GUI can be done either locally or using a AAA server such as the RADIUS or TACACS+.

You can configure WLC for RADIUS authentication by going to Configuration > AAA > Add (a server within the server/group tab). If you multiple RADIUS servers, you can group them using the server group tab. You can also use WLC CLI to configure a remote AAA server.

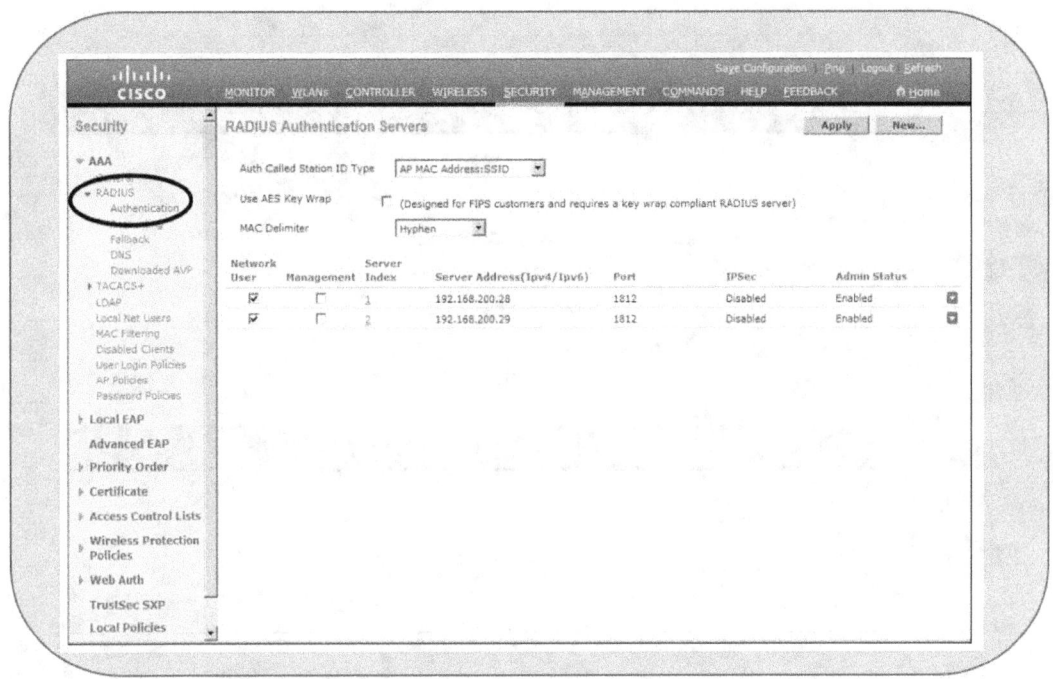

Configure the components of a wireless LAN access for client connectivity using GUI only such as WLAN creation, security settings, QoS profiles, and advanced WLAN settings

You can create a WLAN by going to the WLANs > Create New. You will be prompted to enter WLAN type, profile name, SSID and an ID #.

Once you hit the Apply button, you will be prompted to configure a set of parameters on the next page. Using these parameters, you can configure general parameters (security policies, radio policy, broadcast SSID, etc.) security parameters, QoS, policy-mapping and some advanced parameters. Cisco WLCs offer several L2 WLAN security options.

Security Option	Explanation
None	Open authentication
WPA+WPA2	WPA or WPA2
802.1x	EAP authentication
Static WEP	WEP key-based security
Static WEP + 802.1x	EAP authentication or static WEP
CKIP	Cisco Key Integrity Protocol (CKIP)
None + EAP Passthrough	Open authentication with remote EAP authentication

You can configure QoS options using the QoS tab. You can choose your QoS class, AVC profile, NetFlow monitor, CAC options.

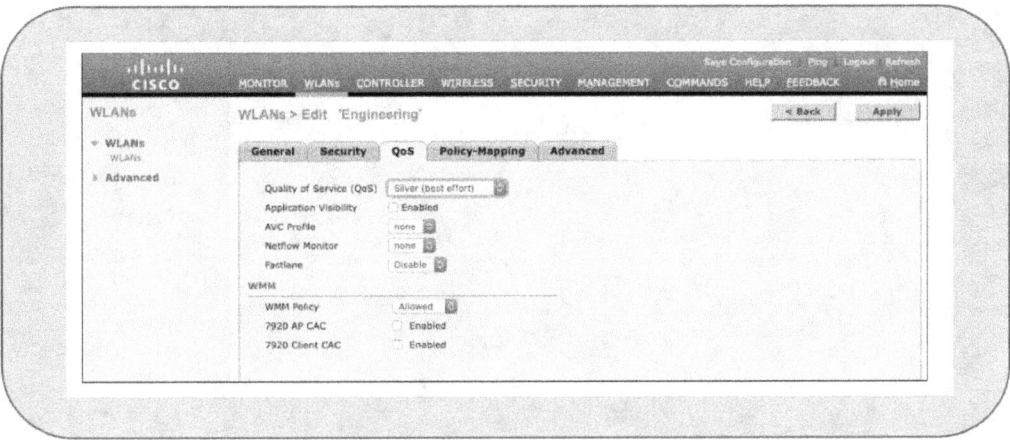

Finally, under the Advanced tab, you will see several WLAN settings such as coverage hole detection, peer-to-peer app blocking, client exclusion, client load limits, etc.

Once you're done with settings in each of the WLAN configuration tabs, you can click Apply button to save and apply your configuration.

Further Reading

https://bit.ly/2CsAKPZ

Chapter Summary

- Virtual LAN (or VLAN) is a broadcast domain that is partitioned virtually to carve out an isolated L2 segment.
- An access port is a port on a switch that is used to transmit data to and from a specific access VLAN connected to an endpoint such as server or a VM
- Any traffic coming on a switch trunk port (ethernet port connecting a switch to another) that is not tagged with a VLAN ID, will be assigned a native VLAN tag which is VLAN ID 1 for Cisco switches
- The trunk is an L2 feature that uses 802.1Q VLAN tags to multiplex (or trunk) traffic from multiple VLANs on a single physical link
- The native VLAN ID is the VLAN that carries untagged traffic on the trunk ports
- EthernetChannel allows bonding or bundling of up to 8 ethernet links into one logical link
- Root port is a forwarding port that is the best port from a non-root switch or bridge to a root switch.
- PortFast is a Cisco proprietary feature that can help edge ports transition to forwarding states quickly
- Cisco FlexConnect is the go-to model for multiple small remote sites or branches that connect into a central site

CHAPTER 3 IP CONNECTIVITY

This chapter covers the following exam topics from Cisco's official 200-901 V1.0[10] Network Associate (CCNA) exam blueprint.

- Interpret the components of routing table
    - Routing protocol code
    - Prefix
    - Network mask
    - Next hop
    - Administrative distance
    - Metric
    - Gateway of last resort
- Determine how a router makes a forwarding decision by default
    - Longest match
    - Administrative distance
    - Routing protocol metric
- Configure and verify IPv4 and IPv6 static routing
    - Default route
    - Network route
    - Host route
    - Floating static
- Configure and verify single area OSPFv2
    - Neighbor adjacencies
    - Point-to-point
    - Broadcast (DR/BDR selection)
    - Router ID
- Describe the purpose of first hop redundancy protocol

---

[10] https://bit.ly/2PGgv4A

Interpret the components of routing table

Routing protocol code

The memory data structure where the routing information is stored is known as the routing table. Cisco IOS uses specific characters to describe the routing protocol as the source of the routing information within the routing tables. Other vendors, such as Juniper, prefer to display the full names of the routing protocols.

```
Router#show ip ro
Codes: C - connected, S - static, I - IGRP, R - RIP, M - mobile, B - BGP
       D - EIGRP, EX - EIGRP external, O - OSPF, IA - OSPF inter area
       N1 - OSPF NSSA external type 1, N2 - OSPF NSSA external type 2
       E1 - OSPF external type 1, E2 - OSPF external type 2, E - EGP
       i - IS-IS, L1 - IS-IS level-1, L2 - IS-IS level-2, ia - IS-IS inter area
       * - candidate default, U - per-user static route, o - ODR
       P - periodic downloaded static route

Gateway of last resort is not set

O    10.0.0.0/8 [110/782] via 200.1.1.2, 00:00:16, Serial0/1/0
     192.168.1.0/27 is subnetted, 2 subnets
C       192.168.1.0 is directly connected, FastEthernet0/0.1
C       192.168.1.32 is directly connected, FastEthernet0/0.2
     200.1.1.0/30 is subnetted, 1 subnets
C       200.1.1.0 is directly connected, Serial0/1/0
```

Here is a complete list of routing protocol codes used in Cisco IOS XE.

- C: connected
- S: static
- I: IGRP derived
- R: RIP derived
- O: OSPF derived
- E: EGP derived
- B: BGP derived
- I: IS-IS derived

Prefix

Routing table contains the routing entries, which are list of network destinations also known as prefixes or routes. In the above "show ip route" example, the 10.0.0.0/8 and 192.168.1.0/27 are the network prefixes.

Network mask

Network masks are used to divide the IP address space into classes, i.e. Class A, B, C, D, and E. On the other hand, the subnet masks are what used in the network configuration to denote the actual mask being used by the administrator which may or may not be across the major network boundary.

In 192.168.1.0/27, the /27 is the class C IP address where network mask is /24 across the classful boundary but the subnet mask being used is /27. The network or subnet masks are also written in the decimal form where /24 and /27 would be equivalent to 255.255.255.0 and 255.255.255.224 respectively.

Next hop

IP routing routes traffic one hop at a time. In the routing table, the next hop is the IP address of another router (or another L3 device) used to route traffic towards its ultimate destination. In the example, the 200.1.1.2 is the next hop for the network prefix 10.0.0.0/8.

Administrative distance

Administrative distance (or AD) is a number that an IP routing device uses as a tie breaker when selecting a best path, to a given destination, when two or more paths exists from two or more different routing protocols or sources. During this comparison, the lowest AD value always prevails.

Metric

A routing metric is a number calculated by a routing protocol for selecting or rejecting a routing path for forwarding IP traffic. The metric is calculated by the respective routing algorithms with the common goal of determining the optimal route to each destination.

It is not to be confused with administrative distance; AD is used as a tiebreaker *across* routing protocols.

Gateway of last resort

Gateway of last resort or default gateway is a route used by an IP routing device, a router, switch, or a firewall, to route traffic where no known or specific route exists.

Determine how a router makes a forwarding decision by default

Longest match

When a packet comes in, the router uses the destination IP address and tries to match it with one of the network prefixes or destinations that exist in the routing table. The router uses the longest prefix match (where the most bits match) as the most preferred route to use.

Administrative distance

AD values can range from 0 (most preferred) to 255 (least preferred). Every vendor has its own default AD values assigned to each routing protocol however they can be customized by the network engineer as desired. AD is an indication of reliability or a measure of route preference of the given routing source.

Below is a comparison of Cisco and Juniper default AD values.

Routing Source	Cisco AD	Juniper AD
Directly connected interfaces	0	0

Static route with exit interface	1	5
Static route with next-hop IP address	1	5
EIGRP summary route	5	n/a
BGP (Internal/External)	20/200	170/170
EIGRP (Internal/External)	90	n/a
OSPF (Internal/External)	110/150	10
IS-IS (L1/L2 Internal)	115/115	15/18
IS-IS (L1/L2 External)	115/115	160/165
RIP	120	100
Unknown	255	

Both Cisco and Juniper allow one-line configuration to customize a default AD value for a given routing protocol. In order to override the default AD value, you can simply go to routing process or configuration mode, and then issue "distance <new-AD>" or "set protocols <protocol> group <group-number> preference <new-AD>" on Cisco IOS and Juniper Junos OS devices respectively. Please note that there are other ways to change AD values.

For troubleshooting, it is imperative to know the main reasons behind why AD values are modified by the network engineers in the first place. There are three most common reasons that are worth noting here.

- Route redistribution
- Network migration from one routing protocol to another
- Using static route as a backup to an existing IGP route

Routing protocol metric

The lower number represents the better route much like the AD.

Configure and verify IPv4 and IPv6 static routing

Default route

The default route can be set up manually by configuring a next hop for 0.0.0.0/0.0.0.0 prefix. For IPv6, the default route is represented as ::/0.

Router(config)#ip route 0.0.0.0 0.0.0.0 10.10.10.1

Network route

The network route is what represents a network prefix, i.e. a destination that represents more than one hosts.

Router(config)#ip route 10.0.0.0 255.0.0.0 192.168.1.1

Host route

The host route is what represents prefix for one host, i.e. a destination that represents one end station. When configuring a host route, the network mask is set to all 1s, i.e. 255.255.255.255 or /32 to represent the most specific match.

Router(config)#ip route 172.16.1.1 255.255.255.255 10.10.10.1

Floating static

A floating static route is simply a backup to another static or dynamically learned route. It is configured with a larger AD than the primary or most preferred route.

Router(config)#ip route 0.0.0.0 0.0.0.0 10.10.10.2 5

You can verify routes using the "show ip route" command.

Configure and verify single area OSPFv2

Open Shortest Path First (OSPF) protocol is defined in RFC 2328 and based on link-state technology where a link is an interface on an L3 device such as a router. The state of the link is an attribute of that interface and its relationship to its neighbors. The interface attributes relevant to OSPF include the IP address, subnet mask, the type of the network, the routers that are also connected to that network and what have you.

Unlike distance vector protocols that use Bellman-Ford, OSPF uses the shortest path first (or SPF or Dijkstra SPF) algorithm to determine the shortest to all known destination networks with the help of a graph.

When an OSPF router boots up, it generates a link-state advertisement (or LSA) for that router which represents the state of links. All routers exchange their LSAs via flooding mechanism. Once an exchange is completed, every router ends up with a database that is used to calculate the shortest path to each destination. Each OSPF router uses the Dijkstra SPF algorithm to derive the shortest path tree and the result of this calculation is stored in the routing table (or RIB). The algorithm places each router at the root of a tree and then calculates the shortest path to each destination network based on the cumulate cost needed to reach that destination.

	EIGRP	**OSPF**
Best Path Selection Algorithm	DUAL FSM	Dijkstra SPF
Administrative Distance	90	110
Metric	Bandwidth, Load, Delay and Reliability	Cost
VLSM	Supported	Not Supported
Authentication	Supported	Supported
Multi Path	Supported	Supported (ECMP)

Open Industry Standard	No	Yes, RFC 2328

OSPF uses interface cost as its metric, which is inversely proportional to the bandwidth of that interface, i.e. higher bandwidth means lower cost by default unless you modify it using ip ospf cost <value> command.

OSPF uses flooding to exchange link-state advertisements between routers and all routers within an area have an exact link-state database. Routers that have interfaces in multiple areas including backbone are known as Area Border Routers (ABRs). Routers that act as a gateway between OSPF and other routing protocols or other instances of the OSPF process are known as Autonomous System Border Routers (or ASBRs). OSPF finite state machine (or FSM) includes eight different states including down, attempt, init, two-way, exstart, exchange, loading and full.

OSPF addresses three classes of network types, point to point (p2p), point to multipoint (p2mp) and broadcast.

Multiple Areas

Enabling OSPF on a Cisco router involves several steps.

1. Enabling an OSPF process (router ospf <process-id>)
2. Assigning areas to the interfaces (network <network/IP-address> <mask> <area-id>)
3. Configuring authentication (optional)

The OSPF process ID is a numeric value only locally significant to the router, i.e. it is never sent to the other routers and thus doesn't have to match with process IDs on other routers either. Technically, you can also run multiple OSPF processes on the same router too.

The network command is a way of assigning an interface to an area whereas a mask is used for ease of configuration so that you can put a bunch of interfaces into an area with one line. Area-id is the area number you want the interface to be in. It can be configured in a simple number format such as 0 or 1 or 2, and in the form of an IP address say 0.0.0.0 or 1.1.1.1.

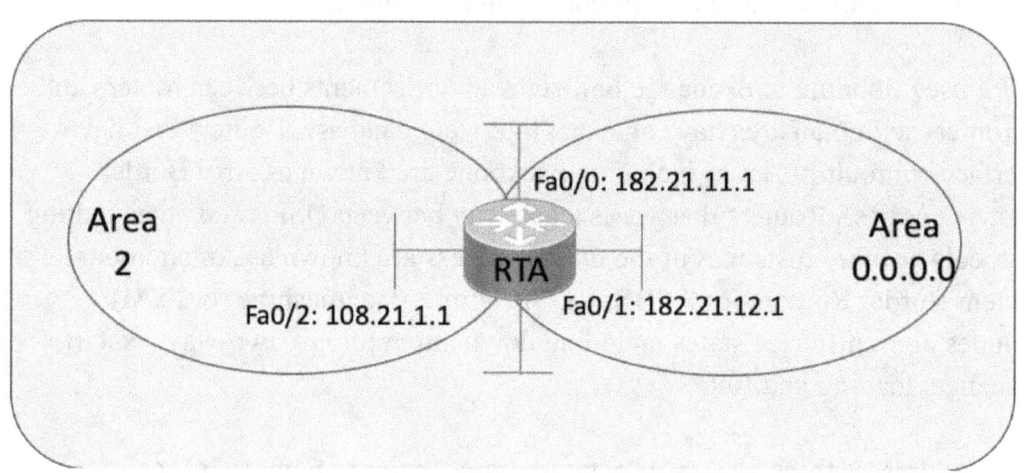

RTA#
interface fa0/0
ip address 182.21.11.1 255.255.255.0

interface fa0/1
ip address 182.21.12.2 255.255.255.0

interface fa0/2
ip address 108.21.1.1 255.255.255.0

router ospf 101
network 182.21.0.0 0.0.255.255 area 0.0.0.0
network 108.21.1.1 0.0.0.0 area 2

Route Summarization

Summarization is about consolidating multiple routes into one single advertisement. In OSPF, this is normally done at the ABRs. You can configure summarization between any two areas, however, it is recommended to summarize towards the backbone area so it can inject those summaries into other areas. Summarization is highly effective if the network addresses assigned are contiguous.

There are two types of summarization, i.e.

- Inter-area routes
- External routes

Inter-area Route Summarization

Inter-area route summarization is done on ABRs and applies to routes from within the AS, i.e. it doesn't apply to routes coming into the OSPF domain from external sources. You can use area <area-id> range <address> <mask> command to configure inter-area summary. Here, area-id refers to the area containing networks that are to be summarized.

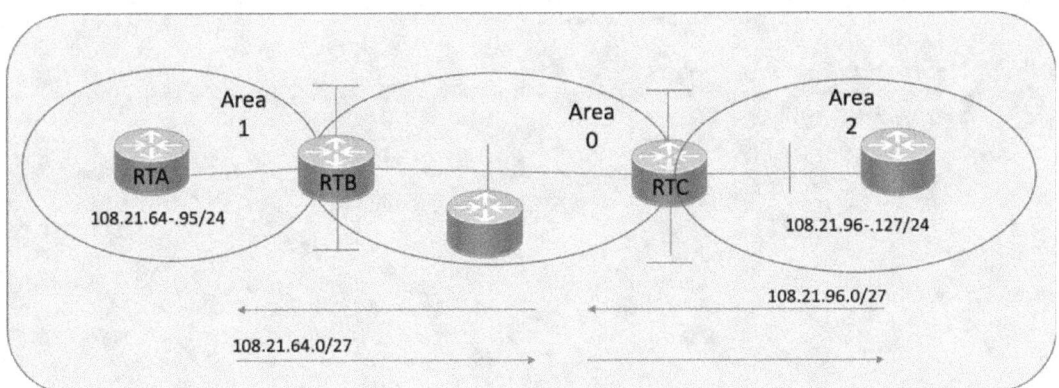

In this topology, RTB is summarizing the range of subnets from 108.21.64.0 to 18.21.95.0 into one range, i.e. 108.21.64.0 255.255.224.0 (/27) into the backbone area. Likewise, RTC is summarizing 108.21.96.0/27 into the backbone.

RTB#
 router ospf 101
 area 1 range 108.21.64.0 255.255.224.0

RTC#
 router ospf 101
 area 1 range 108.21.96.0 255.255.224.0

External Route Summarization

External routes summarization is relevant to external routes only, ones that are injected into OSPF via redistribution. Much like inter-area summarization, the address range being contiguous would make it straightforward.

You will need to use summary-address <ip-address> <mask> command on ASBR(s) doing the redistribution into OSPF. This command will not affect if configured on a router with no connection to another router outside the OSPF domain.

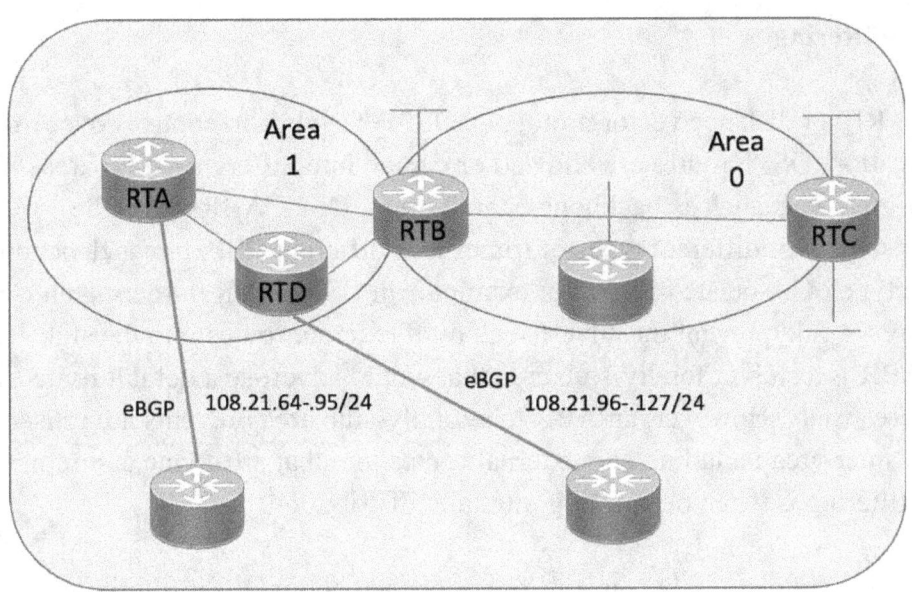

In the above topology, RTA and RTD are injecting external routes into OSPF. RTA is injecting subnets within the range of 108.21.64-95 and RTD is injecting subnets 108.21.96-127.

RTA#
router ospf 101
summary-address 108.21.64.0 255.255.224.0
redistribute bgp 50 metric 1000 subnets

RTD#
router ospf 101
summary-address 108.21.96.0 255.255.224.0
redistribute bgp 20 metric 1000 subnets

Further Reading
OSPF Design Guide[11]

---

[11] https://bit.ly/31jSOUx

Route Filtering

Unlike RIP or distance vector protocols, OSPF has built-in controls over route propagation. OSPF routes are allowed or denied into different OSPF areas based on the area type, such as backbone or stub areas. OSPF ABRs limit the advertisement of different types of routes into different OSPF areas depending on the type of associated LSA. For example, an OSPF ABR bordering an OSPF stub area would prevent the advertisement of external routes into the stub area. The ABR is a stub or totally-stub area that would advertise a default route as an inter-area route. However, an ABR to a totally-stub area prevents advertisements of any inter-area including any external routes into that area. One common use of route filtering is when performing mutual redistribution.

There are a couple of key concepts to understand about OSPF filtering.

- With passive interface command configured, OSPF doesn't send hellos on an interface. This means that the device wouldn't discover any neighbor on that interface.
- Most filtering tools available do not filter out or remove routes from within the LS database.
- The route filters have no impact on the presence of routes in the routing table beyond the local router, i.e. they are only locally significant.

Distribute-list in works on any OSPF router and would prevent routes from being added to the routing table but routes still get added to the LS database i.e. the downstream neighbors will still have those routes. However, distribute-list out works on an ASBR to filter redistributed routes into other protocols.

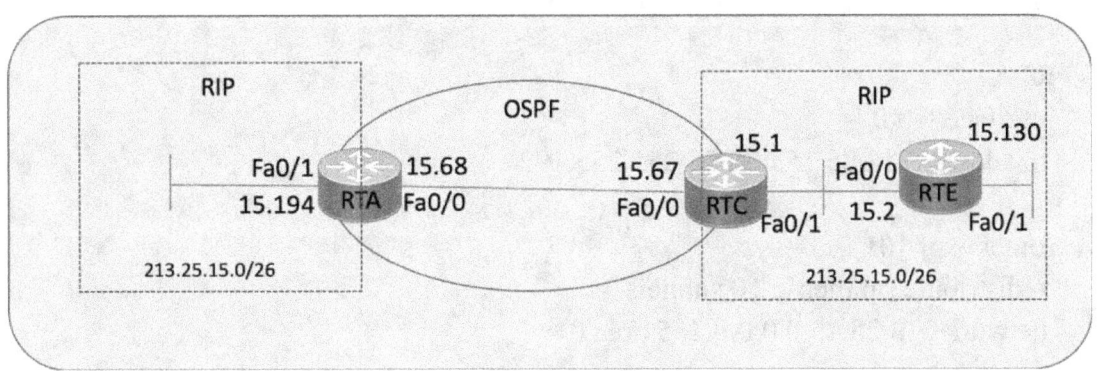

RTE#
 interface fa0/1
  ip address 213.25.15.130 255.255.255.192

 interface fa0/0
  ip address 213.25.15.2 255.255.255.192

 router rip
  network 213.25.15.0

RTC#
 interface fa0/0
  ip address 213.25.15.67 255.255.255.192

 interface fa0/1
  ip address 213.25.15.1 255.255.255.192

 router ospf 101
  redistribute rip metric 10 subnets
  network 213.25.15.0 0.0.0.255 area 0

 router rip
  redistribute ospf 101 metric 2
  passive-interface Ethernet0
  network 213.25.15.0

```
RTA#
interface fa0/0
 ip address 213.25.15.68 255.255.255.192

router ospf 101
 redistribute rip metric 10 subnets
 network 213.25.15.0 0.0.0.255 area 0

router rip
 redistribute ospf 101 metric 1
 network 213.25.15.0
```

If you were to do a show ip route on RTC, you would have found two paths to the 213.25.15.128 destination network. This occurred because RTC advertised the route to RTA via OSPF and RTA advertised it back via RIP. Now, in order to fix this issue, the most effective way would be to use a distribute-list on RTA to deny the 213.25.15.0 network from being put back into RIP.

```
RTA#
 interface fa0/0
 ip address 213.25.15.68 255.255.255.192

 router ospf 101
  redistribute rip metric 10 subnets
  network 213.25.15.0 0.0.0.255 area 0

 router rip
  redistribute ospf 101 metric 1
  network 213.25.15.0
  distribute-list 1 out ospf 101
```

Further Reading
OSPF Configuration Guide[12]

Describe the purpose of first hop redundancy protocol

The purpose of the default gateway redundancy or first-hop redundancy is to help protect against a single node failure so that traffic from end hosts can continue flowing through active default gateway device after a small sub-second convergence.

In the hierarchical design that we have discussed so far, distribution switches define the L2/L3 network boundary and act as the default gateway to the entire L2 domain facing the access layer. Without some form of redundancy in place, default gateway failure could result in a massive outage.

HSRP, VRRP, and GLBP are three popular first-hop redundancy protocols for implementing default gateway redundancy. HSRP and GLBP are Cisco proprietary, whereas VRRP is an IETF standard based protocol defined in RFC 3768 and RFC 5798.

HSRP and VRRP are the recommended protocols and can provide sub-second failover with some tuning for redundant distribution switches. If you are using Cisco switches, best practices indicate that you would be better off using feature rich HSRP however VRRP is a must when your design requires vendor inter-op.

The configuration snippet below shows how you can use HSRP in an enterprise campus deployment and achieve sub-second failover times.

```
interface Vlan100
description Data VLAN for Access-Switch
ip address 10.1.1.1 255.255.255.0
ip helper-address 10.1.2.1
standby 1 ip 10.1.1.2
standby 1 timers msec 200 msec 750
standby 1 priority 150
```

[12] https://bit.ly/2GMcKGh

standby 1 preempt
standby 1 preempt delay minimum 180

It is strongly recommended to configure HSRP with a preemption feature which allows a previously failed device to reclaim its role upon recovery. It is the desired behavior because STP/RSTP root should be the same device as the HSRP primary device for a given subnet or VLAN. Without consolidating HSRP primary and STP root in a single device, the transit link between the distribution switches can act as a transit link where traffic to/from default gateway takes multiple L2 hops. It is also recommended that preemption delay is set to 150% of the time that it takes for the switch to boot up from scratch.

HSRP preemption needs to be configured with switch boot time and overall connectivity to the rest of the network. If preemption and neighbor adjacency occur before switch has L3 connectivity to the core, no traffic will actually and remain blackholed until complete L3 connectivity is restored.

GLBP protects traffic against device or circuit failure much like HSRP or VRRP, but in addition to that, it also allows packet load sharing between a group of redundant routers. Before GLBP, you could only implement HSRP or VRRP hacks to get load balancing to work. For example, you could configure distributes devices as alternate root switches and divide and direct traffic from VLANs into both. Yet another hack would have been to use multiple HSRP groups on a single interface and use DHCP to alternate between the default gateways. As you can see, none of these hacks are clean and could very easily become an administrative nightmare.

HSRP uses a virtual IP and MAC pair which is always assumed by the active router whereas GLBP uses one virtual IP address for multiple virtual MAC addresses.

The configuration snippet below shows GLBP configuration.

interface Vlan100

description Data VLAN for Access-Switch
ip address 10.1.1.1 255.255.255.0
ip helper-address 10.1.2.1
glbp 1 ip 10.1.1.2
glbp 1 timers msec 250 msec 750
glbp 1 priority 150
glbp 1 preempt delay minimum 180

Let's now wrap up the FHRP discussion with a side by side comparison table.

	HSRP	**VRRP**	**GLBP**
Interop	Cisco proprietary	IETF standard	Cisco proprietary
Redundancy mechanism	Active / Standby	Active / Standby	Active / Active
Preemption	Supported, disabled by default	Supported, enabled by default	Supported, enabled by default
Multicast address for hellos	224.0.0.2/224.0.0.102	224.0.0.18	224.0.0.102
Transport	UDP 1985	IP (Protocol #112)	UDP 3222

FHRP Best Practices

- VRRP is an IETF standard and that makes it viable in multivendor networks
- With GLBP, you can go a step beyond and achieve uplink load balancing
- Consider tuning preempt timers to avoid blackholing traffic

HSRP Configuration

R1#sh run int fa0/0

```
Building configuration...
Current configuration : 192 bytes
!
interface FastEthernet0/0
ip address 192.168.1.2 255.255.255.0
duplex auto
speed auto
standby 1 ip 192.168.1.1
standby 1 priority 105
standby 1 preempt
standby 1 track Serial0/0
end

R2#sh run int fa0/0
Building configuration...
Current configuration : 168 bytes
!
interface FastEthernet0/0
ip address 192.168.1.3 255.255.255.0
duplex auto
speed auto
standby 1 ip 192.168.1.1
standby 1 preempt
standby 1 track Serial0/0
end
```

HSRP Verification

```
R1#sh standby

FastEthernet0/0 - Group 1

  State is Active
```

2 state changes, last state change 00:02:43

 Virtual IP address is 192.168.1.1

 Active virtual MAC address is 0000.0c07.ac01

   Local virtual MAC address is 0000.0c07.ac01 (v1 default)

 Hello time 3 sec, hold time 10 sec

   Next hello sent in 2.052 secs

 Preemption enabled

 Active router is local

 Standby router is 192.168.1.3, priority 100 (expires in 7.452 sec)

 Priority 105 (configured 105)

   Track interface Serial0/0 state Up decrement 10

 Group name is "hsrp-Fa0/0-1" (default)

R2#sh standby

FastEthernet0/0 - Group 1

 State is Standby

   1 state change, last state change 00:01:34

 Virtual IP address is 192.168.1.1

Active virtual MAC address is 0000.0c07.ac01

   Local virtual MAC address is 0000.0c07.ac01 (v1 default)

  Hello time 3 sec, hold time 10 sec

   Next hello sent in 1.408 secs

  Preemption enabled

  Active router is 192.168.1.2, priority 105 (expires in 7.068 sec)

  Standby router is local

  Priority 100 (default 100)

   Track interface Serial0/0 state Up decrement 10

  Group name is "hsrp-Fa0/0-1" (default)

VRRP Configuration

Configuration on R1 (master)

R1(config)#interface f0/0
R1(config-if)#ip address 10.1.1.1 255.255.255.0
R1(config-if)#no shutdown
R1(config-if)#vrrp 123 ip 10.1.1.100
R1(config-if)#vrrp 123 preempt

Configuration on R2 (backup)

R2(config)#interface f0/0

R2(config-if)#ip address 10.1.1.2 255.255.255.0
R2(config-if)#no shutdown
R2(config-if)#vrrp 123 ip 10.1.1.100
R2(config-if)#vrpp 123 priority 90

VRRP Verification

VRRP status on R1

R1#show vrrp brief
Interface   Grp Pri Time   Own Pre State   Master addr   Group addr
Fa0/0   123 100 3609   Y   Master 10.1.1.1   10.1.1.100

VRRP status on R2

R2#show vrrp brief
Interface   Grp Pri Time   Own Pre State   Master addr   Group addr
Fa0/0   123 90 3648   Y   Backup 10.1.1.1   10.1.1.100

Chapter Summary

- The memory data structure where the routing information is stored is known as the routing table
- Routing table contains the routing entries, which are list of network destinations also known as prefixes or routes
- Network masks are used to divide the IP address space into classes, i.e. Class A, B, C, D, and E.
- Administrative distance (or AD) is a number that an IP routing device uses as a tie breaker when selecting a best path, to a given destination, when two or more paths exists from two or more different routing protocols or sources
- A routing metric is a number calculated by a routing protocol for selecting or rejecting a routing path for forwarding IP traffic
- Gateway of last resort or default gateway is a route used by an IP routing device, a router, switch, or a firewall, to route traffic where no known or specific route exists.
- A floating static route is simply a backup to another static or dynamically learned route. It is configured with a larger AD than the primary or most preferred route
- Open Shortest Path First (OSPF) protocol is defined in RFC 2328 and based on link-state technology where a link is an interface on an L3 device such as a router
- OSPF uses flooding to exchange link-state advertisements between routers and all routers within an area have an exact link-state database
- VRRP is an IETF standard and that makes it viable in multivendor networks
- HSRP uses a virtual IP and MAC pair which is always assumed by the active router whereas GLBP uses one virtual IP address for multiple virtual MAC addresses.

CHAPTER 4 IP SERVICES

This chapter covers the following exam topics from Cisco's official 200-901 V1.0[13] Network Associate (CCNA) exam blueprint.

- Configure and verify inside source NAT using static and pools
- Configure and verify NTP operating in a client and server mode
- Explain the role of DHCP and DNS within the network
- Explain the function of SNMP in network operations
- Describe the use of syslog features including facilities and levels
- Configure and verify DHCP client and relay
- Explain the forwarding per-hop behavior (PHB) for QoS such as classification, marking, queuing, congestion, policing, shaping
- Configure network devices for remote access using SSH
- Describe the capabilities and function of TFTP/FTP in the network

---

[13] https://bit.ly/2PGgv4A

Configure and verify inside source NAT using static and pools

Network Address Translation (or NAT) comes in many different forms, but in all variations, it is still about translating IP addresses with or without the help of TCP/UDP ports. First, there is NAT and Port Address Translation (PAT).

NAT can be configured in two ways, static and dynamic. Static NAT is the simplest form of NAT where only one to one translation of IP addresses is involved. With static NAT, translations forever stay in the translation table and never time out once they are configured by the network admin. In order to remove entries from the translation table, you've to remove the static NAT statements from the configuration.

Dynamic NAT is like static NAT in the sense that it is still one to one NAT i.e. between an inside local and inside global address. However, the mapping of an inside local to an inside global address happens dynamically. For dynamic NAT to work, you must set up a pool of inside global IP addresses. The dynamic entry only stays in the translation table so long as there is some traffic, in the absence of traffic the entries time out.

What if you had more local addresses and less global addresses? Enter PAT. PAT allows a specific UDP or TCP port on a global address to be translated to a specific port on a local address. Static PAT, much like static NAT, is where you specify the translation rules within the configuration. PAT (or NAT overload) is a way to hide an entire RFC 1918 IP address space behind a single public globally routable IP address (it could also be a few global IP addresses as opposed to one!).

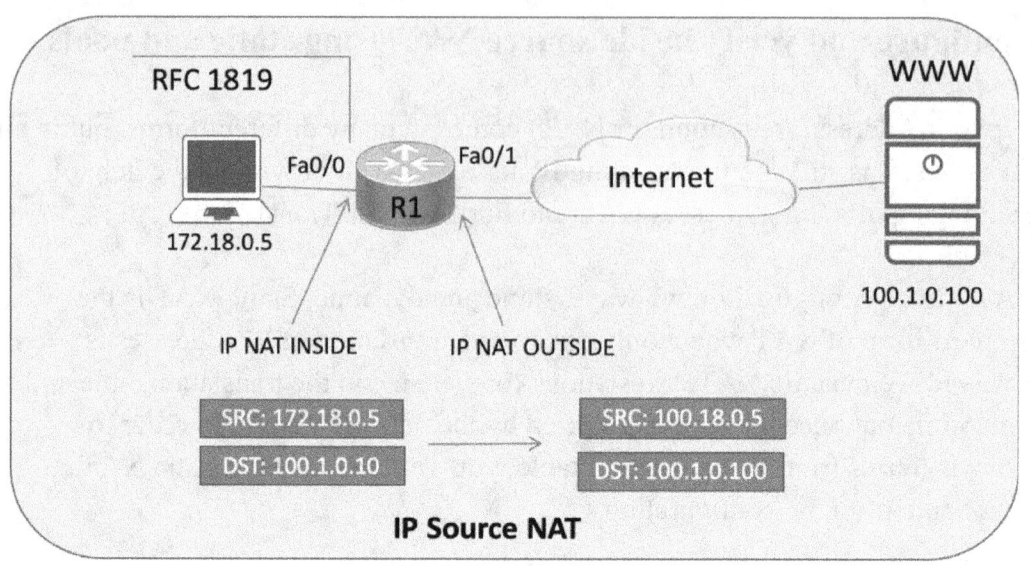

Static NAT

Router(config)#interface fa0/0
Router(config-if)#ip nat inside

Router(config)#interface fa0/1
Router(config-if)#ip nat outside

Router(config)#ip nat inside source static 172.18.0.5 100.18.0.5

Router#sh ip nat translations
Pro   Inside global   Inside local   Outside local   Outside global
 --   100.18.0.5   172.18.0.5   ---   ---

Dynamic NAT

Router(config)#interface fa0/0
Router(config-if)#ip nat inside

Router(config)#interface fa0/1

Router(config-if)#ip nat outside

Router(config)#ip nat pool dynamic-ip 100.0.16.1 100.0.16.6 prefix-length 29
Router(config)#ip access-list standard client-list
Router(config-std-nacl)#permit 172.18.0.0 0.0.0.15
Router(config)#ip nat inside source list client-list pool dynamic-ip

After some traffic matches those NAT rules, you can notice the following.

```
Router#sh ip nat translations
Pro Inside global      Inside local        Outside local       Outside global
icmp 100.16.1:2        172.18.0.1:2        100.1.0.100:2       100.1.0.100:2
tcp 100.16.2:35694     172.18.0.2:35694    100.1.0.100:80      100.1.0.100:80
tcp 100.16.1:56185     172.18.0.1:56185    100.1.0.100:80      100.1.0.100:80
--- 100.16.1           172.18.0.1          ---                 ---
--- 100.16.2           172.18.0.2          ---                 ---
```

Static PAT

Router(config)#interface fa0/0
Router(config-if)#ip nat inside

Router(config)#interface fa0/1
Router(config-if)#ip nat outside

Router(config)#ip nat inside source static tcp 172.17.0.5 80 88.88.88.88 80
Router(config)#ip nat inside source static tcp 172.17.0.6 22 88.88.88.88 666

```
Router#sh ip nat translations
Pro Inside global       Inside local        Outside local       Outside global
tcp 88.88.88.88:80      172.18.0.5:80       ---                 ---
tcp 88.88.88.88:666     172.18.0.6:22       ---                 ---
```

PAT (NAT Overload)

Router(config)#interface fa0/0
Router(config-if)#ip nat inside

Router(config)#interface fa0/1
Router(config-if)#ip nat outside

Router(config)#ip access-list standard client-list
Router(config-std-nacl)#permit 172.18.0.0 0.0.0.255
Router(config)#ip nat inside source list client-list interface fastethernet0/1 overload

After some traffic matches the PAT rules, you can witness the following.

Router#show ip nat translations
Pro Inside global   Inside local   Outside local   Outside global
tcp 88.88.88.88:7921   172.18.0.2:7921   95.100.96.233:443   95.100.96.233:443
tcp 88.88.88.88:8651   172.18.0.5:8651   173.194.44.18:80   173.194.44.18:80
tcp 88.88.88.88:8652   172.18.0.111:8652 173.194.44.18:443   173.194.44.18:443
tcp 88.88.88.88:8653   172.18.0.223:8653 173.194.70.84:443   173.194.70.84:443
udp 88.88.88.88:64116 172.18.0.222:64116 8.8.8.8:53   8.8.8.8:53
udp 88.88.88.88:64756 172.18.0.223:64756 8.8.4.4:53   8.8.4.4:53

Configure and verify NTP operating in a client and server mode

NTP is designed to synchronize the time on a network. It uses UDP to transport packets. An NTP network receives its time from an authoritative time source such as an atomic clock attached to a time server. NTP distributes this time across the network.

NTP client makes a transaction with its server each polling interval. It uses the concept of a stratum to describe the distance in hops between a machine and an authoritative time source. Devices running NTP prefer another device that has the lowest stratum number. Generally, it is possible to achieve 10ms drift over long distances (WAN) and 1ms for LAN.

NTP servers associate with each other in one of three modes.
1. Client/server
2. Active/Passive
3. Broadcast

The Client/server is the most common internet use case. In this setup, a client or dependent server can be synchronized to a group member, but no group member can synchronize to the client or dependent server.

Symmetric Active/passive is useful for configurations where a group of low stratum peers operates as backups for each other.

Broadcast or multicast mode is where clients can be configured to use broadcast or multicast modes. It allows clients to use a single configuration to associate with multiple servers.

Explain the role of DHCP and DNS within the network

The Dynamic Hosting Configuration Protocol (or DHCP) is one of the many network management protocols used on IP networks, typically running on a server, dynamically assigns IPv4 addresses and other related network configurations (such as subnet mask, gateway IP address, etc.) to each device on that network. DHCP is a client/server protocol, where the client is the device that needs an IP address assignment and the server is the entity that governs the assignment being sought.

Domain Name System (or DNS) is a network name management protocol organized in a hierarchical and decentralized fashion to resolve IP device names to their IP addresses. When you browse a website say www.tesla.com, it is a series of DNS servers that help resolve it to its IP address e.g. 209.133.79.61. The series of name servers involved in fully resolving www.tesla.com into the corresponding IP address or addresses would typically include four servers. All DNS communication, by default, takes place in cleartext.

It starts with the DNS recursor (aka DNS resolver) which makes further DNS queries on the client's (in this case PC with the browser) behalf. Recursor will contact the root server which points to an even more specific location, i.e. TLD server. TLD server, in this case, will be one for ".com" domains. The final name server is the authoritative server, and typically the proverbial buck stops here because this name server has access to the requested record and it will simply return the IP address for the given hostname (www.tesla) back to the DNS precursor that made the initial request as far as DNS hierarchy is concerned. DNS is also a client/server protocol.

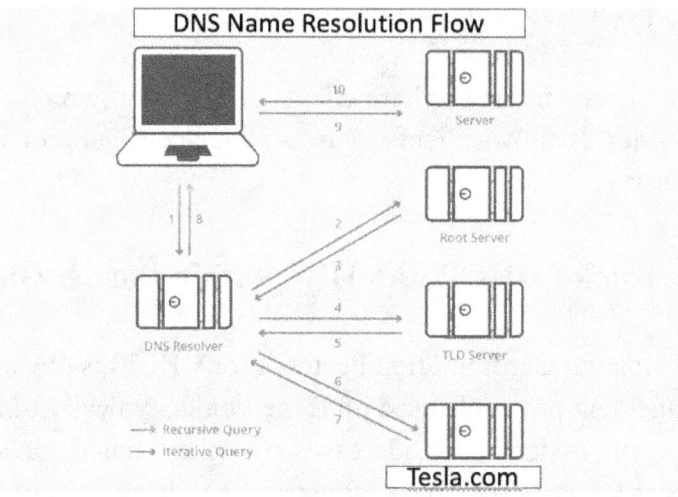

```
MAK1-MBP:~ afaqkhan$ nslookup www.tesla.com
Server:         192.168.1.1
Address:        192.168.1.1#53

Non-authoritative answer:
www.tesla.com   canonical name = www.tesla.com.edgekey.net.
www.tesla.com.edgekey.net       canonical name = e1792.dscx.akamaiedge.net.
Name:   e1792.dscx.akamaiedge.net
Address: 184.30.231.116
```

Explain the function of SNMP in network operations

Simple Network Management Protocol (or SNMP) is an IP protocol responsible for collecting and organizing, in a tree-like fashion, information about the devices being managed. It can also be used to modify those objects to change a device's behavior. It uses UDP ports 161 and 162.

SNMP has been around for over 30 years. Over this time, it has been the de-facto way to monitor networks. It worked great when networks were small and polling a device every 15-30 minutes met operational requirements. SNMP MIBs are a type of data model defining a collection of information that is organized in a hierarchical format that is used along with SNMP. Anyhow, SNMP did work great for monitoring devices say every few minutes, but it never caught on for configuration management purposes due to involvement of custom or proprietary MIBs.

In addition to SNMP, there has always been the network command line interface or CLI. Access to the CLI happens via console, Telnet, or SSH, and it has been the de-facto way of managing configuration of networking devices for the past 20+ years. If you tally up the way devices have been managed for 20 years, you can see that there has been no good way to handle machine to machine mechanism i.e. using software to configure network devices.

SNMPv2c is identical to SNMPv1 except it expands the counters to 64-bit (4.29B) long. This helps a lot with avoiding overlap when working with high speed interfaces. SNMPv3 adds a layer of security to SNMPv2c by adding both authentication and encryption which can be used together or one at a time.

SNMPv3 authentication provides security for SNMP traps, so as messages are created they are assigned a special key that is based on the EngineID of the entity. This key is also shared with the receiver or the management workstation to verify the message integrity. SNMPv3 also provides encryption so SNMP traps can't be modified while in transit to the receiver.

Describe the use of syslog features including facilities and levels

It is Cisco's recommended best practice to configure timestamping on all the routers involved in debugging, since it makes it easier to corroborate log entries across routers.

Logging <syslog-server-IP-address> allows you to configure syslog-based logging on a Cisco router. You can also specify multiple syslog destinations.

Logging trap <level #> command specifies the type of messages by severity level that you want to be sent to the syslog server. The default severity is informational (#6) and lower which includes Debug output (#7). However, you can configure it to be all the way down to 0 which essentially means sent everything to syslog so obviously proceed with caution.

Logging facility <facility-type> lets you specify the facility level used by the syslog. The default is local7 whereas possible values go from local0 to local7.

Router#config terminal
Enter configuration commands, one per line. End with CNTL/Z.
Router(config)#logging 192.168.1.10
Router(config)#service timestamps debug datetime localtime show-timezone msec
Router(config)#service timestamps log datetime localtime show-timezone msec
Router(config)#logging facility local4

Router(config)#logging trap warning
Router(config)#end

Verifying Syslog

You can verify syslog by using the "show logging" command.

Router#show logging
Syslog logging: enabled (0 messages dropped, 0 flushes, 0 overruns)
    Console logging: level debugging, 79 messages logged
    Monitor logging: level debugging, 0 messages logged
    Buffer logging: disabled
    Trap logging: level warnings, 80 message lines logged
        Logging to 192.168.1.10, 57 message lines logged

Configure and verify DHCP client and relay

Dynamic Host Configuration Protocol (or DHCP) is used for assigning IP addresses to any IP devices that are configured as DHCP clients. By default, the IP address assignment is dynamic however the DHCP server can be configured to hand out a pre-assigned or static IP address based on the device's MAC address.

All Cisco IOS XE devices can server as DHCP servers. During the address assignment, a DHCP server can also be configured to provide DHCP option values. These options can include information such as subnet mask, gateway, NTP server, Hostname, TFTP server name, DHCP relay agent information etc.

In case of DHCPv6, likewise there are a number of options available.

- Vendor specific information option
- TFTP server addresses
- Syslog server addresses
- DNS recursive name server

- FQDN option

DHCP relay agent operates as an interface between DHCP client and the server. It listens for client requests and adds vital configuration data which can be used by the server to allocate the IP address for the client. Likewise, when the DHCP server responds, the relay agent forwards the reply to the DHCP client.

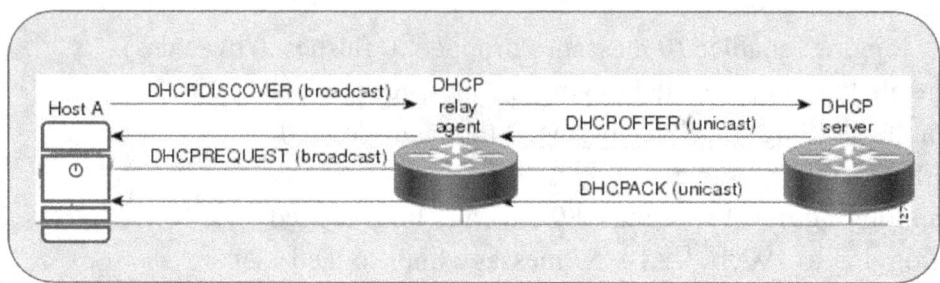

Router (config)#ip dhcp relay enable
Router (config)# ip dhcp relay server 10.10.10.1
Router (config)#ip dhcp relay information policy replace

You can verify DHCP relay agent configuration using any of the following commands.

- Show ip dhcp relay conf
- Show ip dhcp relay information policy
- Show ip dhcp relay statistics

Router# show ip dhcp relay information policy
DHCP Relay reforwarding policy configured = REPLACE

Explain the forwarding per-hop behavior (PHB) for QoS such as classification, marking, queuing, congestion, policing, shaping

Per-hop behavior (PHB) is a term used in DiffServ, essentially it defines the policy and priority applied to a packet when traversing an L3 hop such as a router or a firewall.

In QoS, classification is the process of distinguishing one type of traffic from another based upon ACLs, Differentiated Services Code Point (DSCP), or Class of Service (CoS).

Marking is used to on traffic to convey specific information to a downstream device in the network.

Both Shaping and Policing are the processes of imposing a maximum rate of traffic. With shaping, you can apply lower bitrates than what the physical interface is capable of during the period of traffic congestion. Policing is like shaping; however, the excess bitrate is not buffered but simply dropped.

Queuing is used to manage traffic congestion by sending traffic to specific queues for servicing and scheduling based on bandwidth allocation.

Configure network devices for remote access using SSH

Secure Shell (SSH) is a protocol which provides secure remote access connection to network devices such as routers, switches and firewalls. There are two versions of SSH protocol, SSHv1 and SSHv2. SSHv2 is more secure and thus preferred variant to use for remote access.

SSHv2 encrypts all data which helps protect again eavesdropping. It authenticates the identity of the server where SSH clients validates the server's host key against a local list of available keys that are associated with server names and addresses. SSHv2 can also protect against man-in-the-middle attack by using private/public keys for authentication.

Configuring SSH is straightforward. You need to generate an RSA key pair and configure how to authenticate your users. For authentication, you can use a local or remote AAA server.

aaa new-model
username cciein8weeks password ASD$%^$
line vty 0 4
transport input ssh

ip ssh version 2
crypto key generate rsa

You can connect to an SSH server from a router or from another machine that has an SSH client installed on it. Windows 10 (included but installed by default), macOS and Linux all come with a native SSH client.

On a macOS, you can use the following command to connect from within a Terminal.

Ssh username@ip-address

Ssh cciein8weeks@10.10.10.1

Describe the capabilities and function of TFTP/FTP in the network

FTP is a client/server protocol that can be used to transfer files between two computer systems. Trivial FTP (or TFTP) is yet another file transfer protocol. FTP is secure whereas TFTP is not. FTP uses TCP for protocol transport whereas TFTP uses UDP. FTP uses TCP port 20 and 21 whereas TFTP uses UDP port 69.

SFTP and FTPS are also example of secure file transfer protocols, where SFTP uses SSH and FTPS uses SSL/TLS for authentication and encryption.

Chapter Summary

- NAT can be configured in two ways, static and dynamic.
- Dynamic NAT is like static NAT in the sense that it is still one to one NAT i.e. between an inside local and inside global address
- NTP is designed to synchronize the time on a network
- The Dynamic Hosting Configuration Protocol (or DHCP) is one of the many network management protocols used on IP networks, typically running on a server, dynamically assigns IPv4 addresses and other related network configurations (such as subnet mask, gateway IP address, etc.) to each device on that network
- Domain Name System (or DNS) is a network name management protocol organized in a hierarchical and decentralized fashion to resolve IP device names to their IP addresses
- Simple Network Management Protocol (or SNMP) is an IP protocol responsible for collecting and organizing, in a tree-like fashion, information about the devices being managed
- Logging <syslog-server-IP-address> allows you to configure syslog-based logging on a Cisco router. You can also specify multiple syslog destinations
- Dynamic Host Configuration Protocol (or DHCP) is used for assigning IP addresses to any IP devices that are configured as DHCP clients.
- Per-hop behavior (PHB) is a term used in DiffServ, essentially it defines the policy and priority applied to a packet when traversing an L3 hop such as a router or a firewall
- Secure Shell (SSH) is a protocol which provides secure remote access connection to network devices such as routers, switches and firewalls. There are two versions of SSH protocol, SSHv1 and SSHv2. SSHv2 is more secure and thus preferred variant to use for remote access.

CHAPTER 5 SECURITY FUNDAMENTALS

This chapter covers the following exam topics from Cisco's official 200-901 V1.0[14] Network Associate (CCNA) exam blueprint.

- Define key security concepts (threats, vulnerabilities, exploits, and mitigation techniques)
- Describe security program elements (user awareness, training, and physical access control)
- Configure device access control using local passwords
- Describe security password policies elements, such as management, complexity, and password alternatives (multifactor authentication, certificates, and biometrics)
- Describe remote access and site-to-site VPNs
- Configure and verify access control lists
- Configure Layer 2 security features (DHCP snooping, dynamic ARP inspection, and port security)
- Differentiate authentication, authorization, and accounting concepts
- Describe wireless security protocols (WPA, WPA2, and WPA3)
- Configure WLAN using WPA2 PSK using the GUI

---

[14] https://bit.ly/2PGgv4A

Define key security concepts (threats, vulnerabilities, exploits, and mitigation techniques)

It is crucial to understand that the global cost of a malware is staggering. With cybercrime on the rise, the cost is expected to reach $6T by 2021.

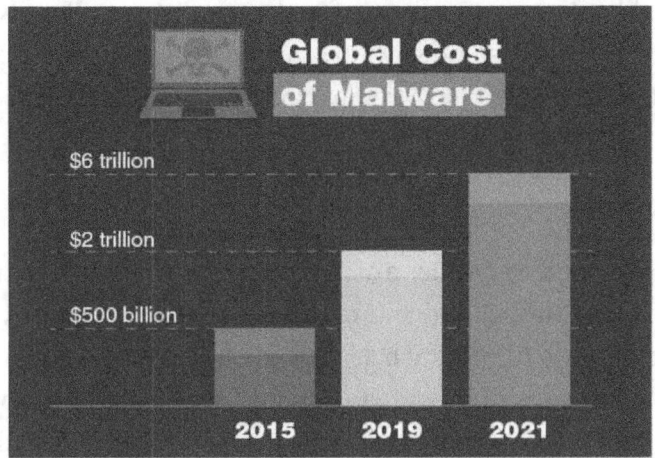

The amount of monetary damage caused by cybercrimes has exponentially risen over the past two decades, surpassing $1.5T today.

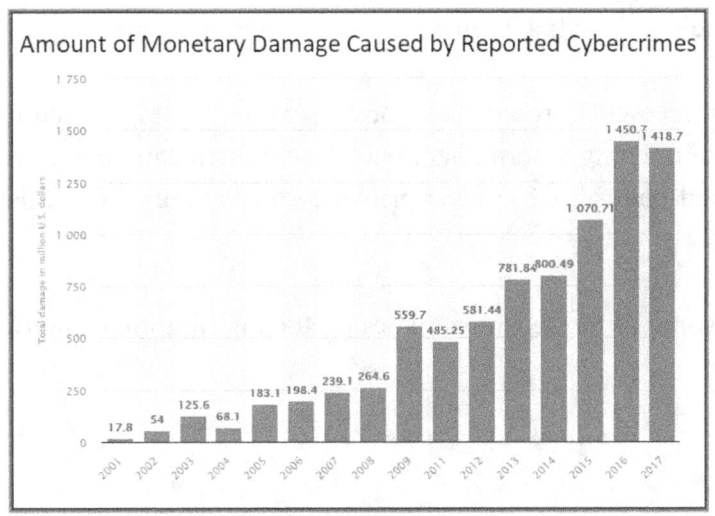

Viruses

The virus is a type of malware attached to another file and can replicate and spread once a user on the target machine executes it. The terms Virus and malware are often used interchangeably, but they don't mean the same thing. Malware is a broad term that is used to describe all sorts of unwanted and malicious code. All viruses are a form of malware, but not all malware are viruses, i.e., malware can also be spyware, trojan, or worm. Viruses are now a thing of the past. Worms are also rare but can't be completely ruled out.

Trojans

A trojan or a trojan horse is neither a virus nor a worm. Unlike a virus, a trojan appears as a bona fide application and requires a user action for execution. Trojans can take various forms, such as free software, or music, even legit apps. If you visit shady websites or download cracked applications or some unknown free programs or any other social engineering method that takes advantage of a recent trend. In late 2017, when Intel announced that most of its x86 processors are vulnerable to Meltdown or Spectre attack, which allowed a rogue process to read all system memory, even when it is not supposed to. Hackers used that panic and released patches (e.g., Smoke loader), which did nothing to fix the problem but helped install a Trojan.

In most recent incidents, trojans have been used to target financial institutions with the aim of opening a permanent backdoor, which can be used to connect to a command-and-control (C2) server primarily for the purposes of data and identity thefts.

Let's review some of the recent statistics on the distribution of malware by type and applications.

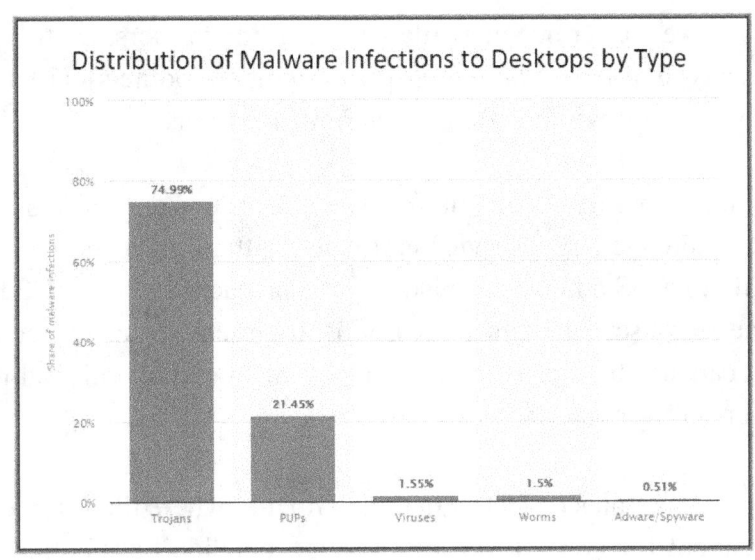

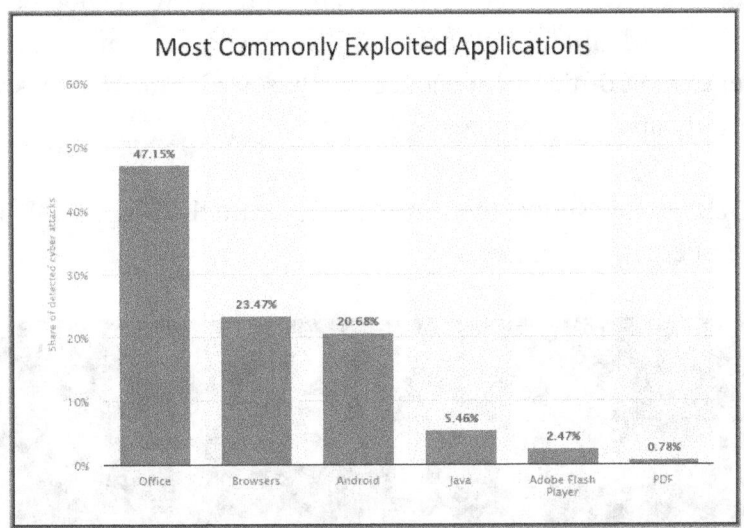

DoS/DDoS Attacks

Denial of Service (or DoS) is a type of cyber-attack in which the attacker tries to disrupt regular traffic directed to a server, service, or even an entire network by overwhelming the target with malicious traffic.

The aim is to make the service unavailable to legitimate users. Distributed DoS (or DDoS) is a type of DoS where multiple systems (or botnets) target a single service and bombard it with traffic from various locations.

There are several types of DDoS attacks. The most prevalent form is a volume-based attack, where the target service is flooded with massive amounts of UDP or ICMP traffic. DDoS attacks can also target a protocol such as TCP by swamping the target service with SYN floods, fragmented packets, etc. The DDoS attack can also be orchestrated by exploiting a certain vulnerability within the application software stack.

The most recent examples of DDoS include GitHub, where the service was flooded with about 1.3 Tbps of traffic. The attackers didn't use botnets but instead exploited vulnerable web servers on the internet with spoofed traffic, which in turn flooded GitHub servers. Despite the enormity of the traffic volume and the clever exploit of the mem cached databases, GitHub services were impacted for only about 20 minutes.

The traffic graph below shows real-time traffic while the biggest DDoS in the history of the internet, was underway.

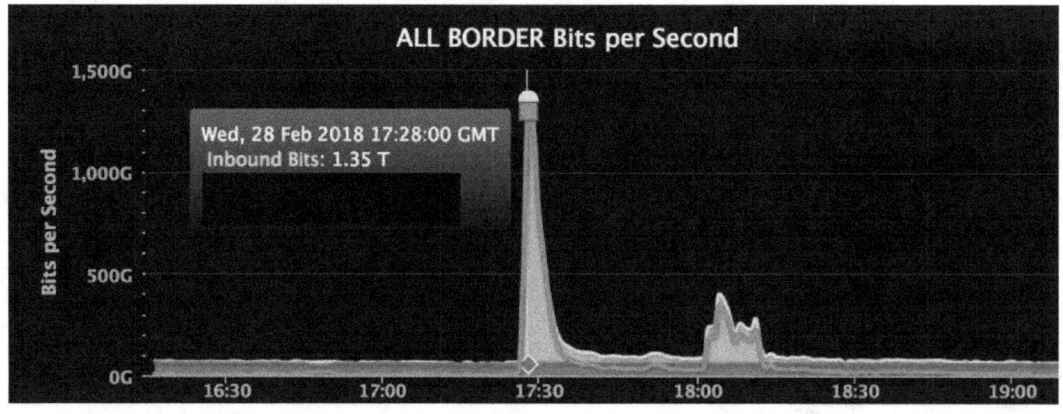

Here is the list of hosting countries with the largest DDoS weapons, China, USA and then Russia make the top three.

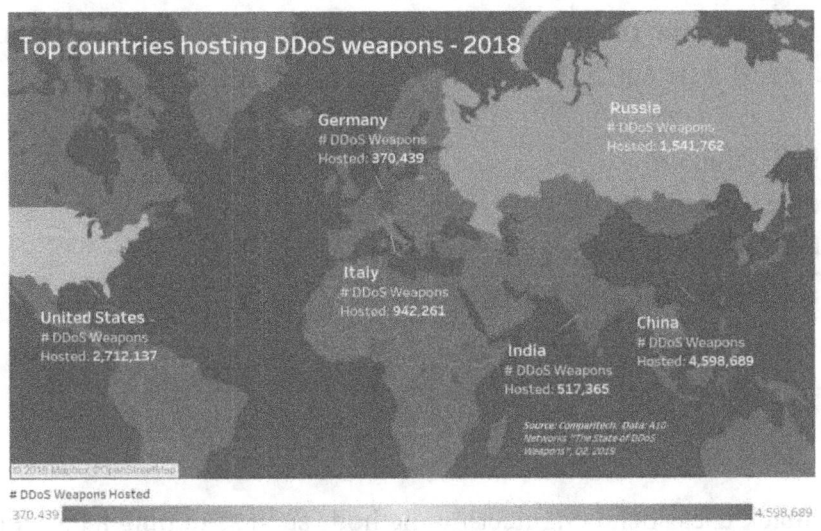

The statistics below shows that large and very large DDoS attacks are on the rise.

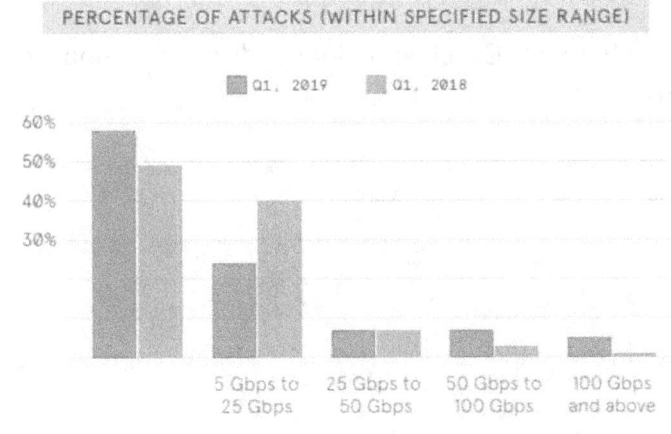

Figure 6 - Comparison of attacks by size Q1, 2019 vs. Q1, 2018

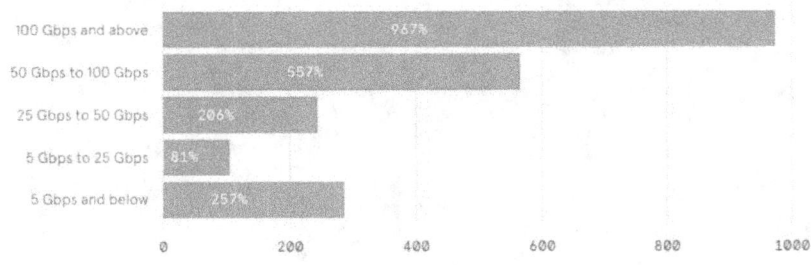

As per A10 Networks, the top 5 BGP ASNs with infected IP addresses include China, Brazil, Russia and S. Korea.

- China Unicom
- China Telecom
- TIM Cellular S.A. (Brazil)
- Rostelecom (Russia)
- Korea Telecom (South Korea)

Phishing

Phishing attack uses social engineering methods such as duping a target into opening an email or a message such as WhatsApp or SMS. When orchestrating phishing attacks, the attacker pretends to be a trusted entity. As per Verizon Data Break Report, 93% of social attacks were phishing related.

It seems Dropbox, Microsoft Excel, and Google drive are amongst the most popular click-baits.

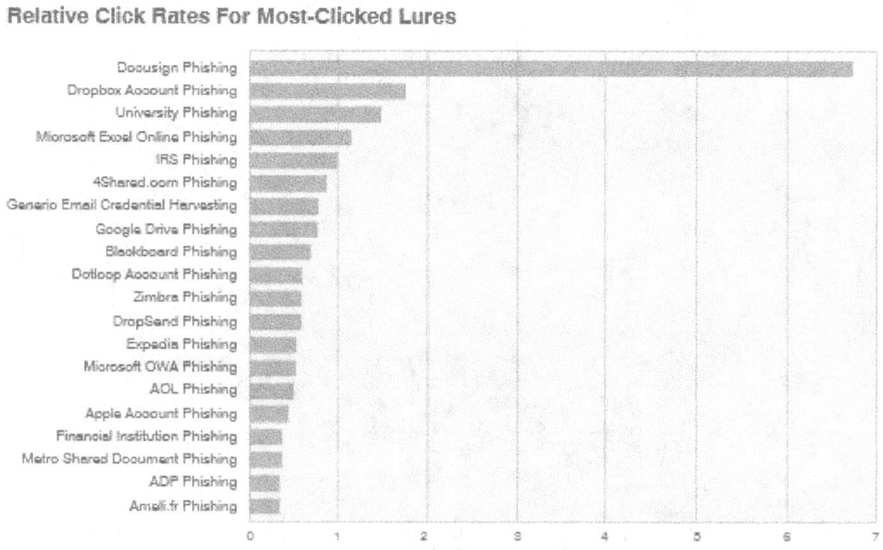

Figure 2: Average click rates for the top 10 lures

Rootkits

Rootkits are a type of malware that remains hidden from other apps on a computer by maintaining privileged access to the OS. Rootkits aim to subvert built-in OS access control by taking advantage of vulnerabilities so it can run without restrictions.

With the ability to hide and run, the attacker can use a rootkit to steal user credentials and provide a full access backdoor that can be used to install more malware. Rootkits often take the form of loadable modules or device drivers.

Man-in-the-Middle (MiTM) Attacks

Man-in-the-Middle (or MiTM) is a type of attack where a perpetrator listens for and alter messages between two parties who believe they are securely communicating with each other. It is a form of active eavesdropping. Most crypto protocols use some of the mutual endpoint authentication to prevent MiTM attacks. The notable instances of MiTM include Comcast injecting JS code to 3rd party web pages with the aim of showing its own ads and messages and NSA's impersonation of Google.

SQL Injection (SQLI)

The SQL injection is a type of attack that uses malicious SQL code and targets a web backend database to get access to information that was not supposed to be displayed. An attacker manipulates a standard SQL query to exploit non-validated inputs to a database.

Let's say we want to display a specific product, such as SCOR course (product #5), from the CCIEin8Weeks.com course catalog. In order to accomplish our goal, we browse to the following URL.

https://www.cciein8weeks.com/courses/courses.asp?courseid=5

Behind the scenes, the web server executes the following SQL query to pull SCOR course information.

SELECT CourseName, CourseDescription
FROM Courses
WHERE CourseNumber = 5

Now, let's say we purposefully modify our URL to the following.

https://www.cciein8weeks.com/courses/courses.asp?courseid=5or3=3

If successful, the corresponding SQL query would look like the following.

SELECT CourseName, CourseDescription
FROM Courses
WHERE CourseNumber = 5 OR 3=3

Since 3 is always equal to 3 or always resolves to TRUE, this may result in displaying course information for all the published or even unpublished or hidden courses.
To take this to the next level, an attacked may attempt to delete the entire User database by padding a semicolon and a "DROP TABLE USERS" to the end of the URL.

You can protect against SQLI attacks by validating or sanitizing input to your SQL database. You may also use a web application firewall (or WAF) to filter out malicious SQL queries.

Cross-site Scripting (XSS)

Cross-site Scripting (or XSS) attacks are a type of injection attack in which an attacker injects malicious code in the form of client-side scripts, which can then be executed and viewed by other users. XSS vulnerability allows attackers to bypass safety controls such as the same-origin policy.

There are three types of XSS attacks.

- Reflected XSS, where the malicious script is contained within the current HTTP transaction. It is a server-side attack.
- Stored XSS, where the malicious script comes from within the webserver's database. It is a server-side attack.
- DOM-based XSS, where the vulnerability lies in the front-end or client-side software

Cross-Site Scripting (or XSS) is by far the most popular type of attack.

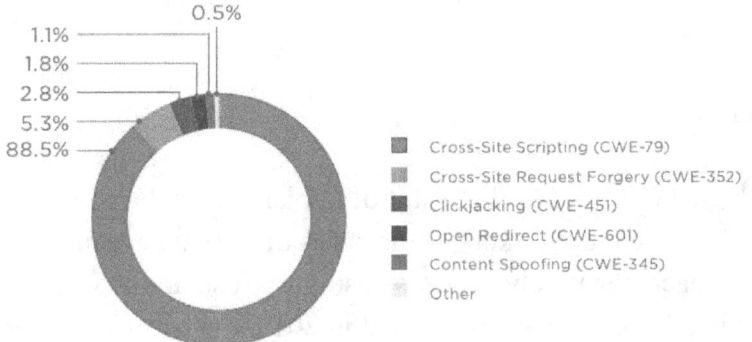

Malware

Malicious software (or the malware) is any software that was written with the malicious intent of damaging, stealing, or extorting. Viruses, trojans, spyware, ransomware, and rootkits are all different forms of malware.

Malware has increased exponentially over the past decade.

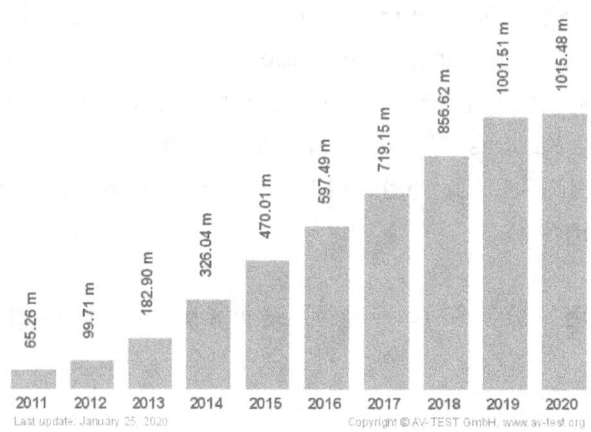

Data Breaches

Cloud data breaches are often the result of human errors than a software vulnerability exploited by hackers. Regardless of the cause, data breaches are costly. Each breach negatively impacts customer trust, and that leads to loss of business. As per an IBM report published in 2019, the cost of an average global data breach has risen to $4M. In the US, on average, has the highest cost pegged at about $8.19M and healthcare sector has the highest average cost of any other industry at $6.45M. Over the past ten years, Microsoft, LinkedIn, Dropbox, and Yahoo has all witnessed data breaches involving user accounts information.

Insecure APIs

Cloud service providers provide the APIs to software developers so they can interface with the cloud services. Cloud APIs are mostly based on REST and SOAP frameworks. In addition to cloud APIs, there can also be some open APIs as well as vendor-specific APIs that help manage various infrastructure resources inside the cloud.

API security is more than just access control since APIs are used to transfer data to and from your cloud resources. Thus, it holds keys to protect against data security and privacy, data leakage, and data integrity. OWASP Top 10 vulnerability report also notes the importance of API security.

Compromised Credentials

Credentials are compromised on a regular basis, and the worst part is that more than half of the companies cannot even detect compromised credentials. Now, let's cover some of the recent hacks where user or account information was stolen.

Year Breach Occurred	Organization	No. of Accounts/Records Compromised
2007	TJ Maxx	94M
2010	Sony PSN	77M
2013	Evernote	50M
2014	eBay	145M
2014	Home Depot	56M
2014	JPMC	76M
2015	Anthem	80M

Describe security program elements (user awareness, training, and physical access control)

Cyber domain consists of four elements, i.e. the physical domain (hardware and software), the information domain (confidentiality, integrity, and availability), the cognitive domain (how information is perceived and analyzed) and the social domain (ethics and the social norms).

User security awareness, as part of the enterprise security policy, includes educating, training and testing employees as part of proactively protecting the business against the cybercrimes such as phishing and other social engineer attack vectors. User security awareness can also protect against malware, ransomware, and spyware.

Physical security protects people, data, equipment, systems, facilities and the enterprise assets. Without physical security controls, most digital defenses could be sidestepped. Physical security protection includes alarm systems, mantraps, and physical intrusion detection systems.

Configure device access control using local passwords

There are two primary ways that you can use to configure the device access control, i.e. local username/passwords and remote Authentication, Authorization, and Accounting (or AAA) servers. Local user database stores credentials within the device's NVRAM where remote AAA is configured on an external host such as a server running RADIUS or TACACS+ software. You can use local database or AAA for authenticating terminal access to a router via Telnet/SSH.

AAA is used by the network admins for controlling access to various network devices (such as FWs, routers, switches) as well as to authorize the commands that an admin can execute during the authenticated session. Command authorization is only supported by the TACACS+ protocol.

AAA is also used for access control by way of downloadable ACLs (or dACLs), which are Access Control Elements (or ACEs) that are downloaded after a session is authenticated and applied to the remote user session.

Configuring login authentication and authorization using a local database on Cisco IOS XE

```
aaa new-model
aaa authorization login default local
line vty 0 4
login authentication default
```

username cciein8weeks password ASd#@$

Configuring login authentication and authorization using a remote RADIUS server on Cisco IOS XE

aaa new-model
radius server radius-cisco-ise
 address ipv4 192.168.1.10
 key cciein8weeks

aaa group server radius radius-cisco-ise-group
 server name radius-cisco-ise

aaa authentication login vty-authentication group radius-cisco-ise-group local
aaa authorization exec vty-authorization group radius-cisco-ise-group local
aaa accounting exec default

line vty 0 4
 authorization exec vty-authorization
 login authentication vty-authentication

Describe security password policies elements, such as management, complexity, and password alternatives (multifactor authentication, certificates, and biometrics)

Password management complexity is a solution that helps manage rules you choose to implement password complexity within your enterprise. You can take your user authentication to another level by implementing two-factor (2FA) or multi-factor authentication (MFA).

All 2FA is MFA, but not all MFA is 2FA, i.e., 2FA is a subset of MFA. MFA is vital because it adds another layer of protection.

MFA involves presenting at least two of the following pieces of evidence.

Knowledge (something you know, like your ATM PIN)
Possession (something you have, like your ATM card)
Inheritance (something you are)

Typical use cases for MFA includes the following.

- Password resets
- Device authorization and management
- Password less authentication
- Identity confirmation

You can use the Cisco Duo solution to deploy MFA to implement zero-trust security for your workplace and workload.

Describe remote access and site-to-site VPNs

Cisco supports many site-to-site VPN solutions.

	Static VTI	**Dynamic VTI**	**Crypto Map**	**DMVPN**	**FlexVPN**
Solution Protocol Stack	IKEv1/v2, IPsec	IKEv1/v2, IPsec	IKv1/v2, IPsec, IPsec/p2pGRE	IKEv1/v2, IPsec, p2p/p2mp GRE, NHRP	IKEv2, IPsec, p2p/p2mp GRE, NHRP
Primary Use Case	Site to site tunnels	Site to site, client to site	Site to site	Site to site, hub/spoke	Site to site, hub/spoke
Ease of Configuration	Easy	Easier	Complex at scale	Easier at scale	Easiest at scale
HA Support	Box to box with routing protocol	Box to box with routing protocol	Box to box with GRE and routing protocols	Dual Hub	Dual Hub

AnyConnect Support	No	Yes	Yes	No	Yes

All VPN solutions have their pros and cons and thus tailored for specific scenarios.

	P2P IPSec (static VTI or crypto map)	Dynamic VTI or p2p GRE over IPSec	DMVPN	GETVPN	FlexVPN
Support for unicast traffic encryption	Yes	Yes	Yes	Yes	Yes
Support for multicast traffic encryption	No	Yes	Yes	Yes	Yes
Support for Group encryption	No	No	No	Yes	No
Support for VPN client	No	Yes	No	No	Yes
Keying protocol	IKEv1/v2	IKEv1/v2	IKEv1/v2	IKEv1/GDOI IKEv2/GDOI	IKEv2
NHRP use	No	No	Spoke to spoke and spoke to hub	No	Spoke to spoke only

GRE can be configured in both point to point (or p2p) or point to multipoint (or p2mp) modes with IPsec. Here is the breakdown of a preferred GRE/IPsec configuration for various topologies.

Topology Type	IPSec Solution	GRE Mode
Site to Site	Crypto Map (IPSec Tunnel mode)	P2p

Hub and Spoke / Spoke to Spoke	1. Single Tier: DMVPN (IPSec Transport mode) 2. Dual Tier: DMVPN (IPSec Tunnel mode) 3. Dynamic VTI	P2mp /w NHRP (DMVPN)
Full Mesh	GETVPN (Cisco Proprietary)	N/A

In this example, we will use a crypto map configuration for IPSec without GRE.

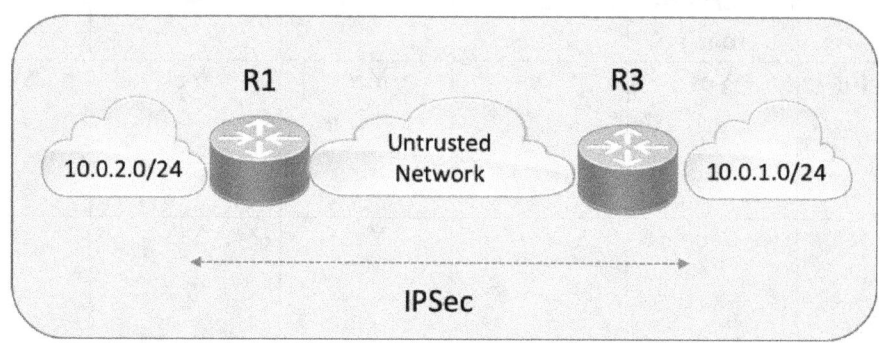

On R1:

R1(config)# crypto isakmp policy 10
R1(config-isakmp)# hash md5
R1(config-isakmp)# authentication pre-share
R1(config-isakmp)# group 2
R1(config-isakmp)# encryption 3des

R1(config)# crypto isakmp key cisco address 100.10.10.1

Rx(config)# crypto ipsec transform-set SAMPLE esp-des esp-md5-hmac

R1(config)# access-list 101 permit ip 10.0.2.0 0.255.255.255 10.0.1.0 0.0.0.255

R1(config)# crypto map SAMPLE 10 ipsec-isakmp
R1(config-crypto-map)# set peer 100.10.10.1
R1(config-crypto-map)# match address 101
R1(config-crypto-map)# set transform-set SAMPLE

R1(config)# interface giga0/1
R1(config-if)#IP address 100.10.10.2 255.255.255.0
R1(config-if)# crypto map SAMPLE

On R3:

R3(config)# crypto isakmp policy 10
R3(config-isakmp)# hash md5
R3(config-isakmp)# authentication pre-share
R3(config-isakmp)# group 2
R3(config-isakmp)# encryption 3des

R3(config)# crypto isakmp key cisco address 100.10.10.2
R3(config)# crypto ipsec transform-set SAMPLE esp-des esp-md5-hmac
R1(config)# access-list 101 permit ip 10.0.1.0 0.0.0.255 10.0.2.0 0.255.255.255

R3(config)# crypto map SAMPLE 10 ipsec-isakmp
R3(config-crypto-map)# set peer 100.10.10.2
R3(config-crypto-map)# match address 101
R3(config-crypto-map)# set transform-set SAMPLE

R3(config)# interface giga0/1
R1(config-if)#IP address 100.10.10.2 255.255.255.0
R3(config-if)# crypto map SAMPLE

Verifying GRE/IPSec Configuration

To verify and troubleshoot IPSec or GRE/IPSec configuration, you can use any of the following Cisco IOS CLIs.

Show crypto isakmp sa, displays ISAKMP or IKE SA details.
Show crypto ipsec sa, displays IPSec SA details.
Show ip interface brief, displays list of all interfaces.

Configure and verify access control lists

Access lists (or ACLs) are stateless L2-L4 packet filters to specify what should be permitted and denied inbound or outbound to and from a network. As a reference, firewalls are stateful packet filters and can operate from L2 to L7 packet headers or data.

ACLs configuration requires three pieces of information, i.e.

1. Network or IP address (to be permitted or blocked)
2. Reverse mask (for ease of configuration)
3. Direction (inbound or outbound or both)

ACL Configuration

```
router#configure terminal
 Enter configuration commands, one per line.  End with CNTL/Z.
 router(config)#access-list 101 deny icmp any any
 router(config)#access-list 101 permit ip any any
 router(config)#^Z
```

```
router#configure terminal
 Enter configuration commands, one per line.  End with CNTL/Z.
 router(config)#no access-list 101 deny icmp any any
 router(config)#^Z

 router#show access-list
 router#
  *Mar  9 00:43:29.832: %SYS-5-CONFIG_I: Configured from console by console
```

ACL Verification

```
router#show access-list
Extended IP access list 101
   deny icmp any any
   permit ip any any
router#
```

Further Reading
ACL Configuration Guide[15]

Configure Layer 2 security features (DHCP snooping, dynamic ARP inspection, and port security)

DHCP snooping is an L2 security feature where a switch filters out untrusted DHCP messages based on a DHCP snooping binding table. For DHCP snooping to work, all DHCP servers must be connected to the switch on the trusted interface. When a switch receives a packet on an untrusted interface with DHCP snooping enabled for the VLAN, the switch compares the source MAC and the DHCP client MAC, if the two addresses match, the switch forwards the packet otherwise it drops the packet.

To enable DHCP snooping, you first need to enable it globally, and then on the VLAN where the switch needs to snoop for rogue DHCP traffic.

Dynamic ARP Inspection (DAI)

Dynamic ARP Inspection (or DAI) is another L2 security feature that validates ARP packets. Each IP host maintains an ARP cache that contains IP to MAC bindings. Now, since ARP requests are broadcast by nature, all hosts on an L2 segment receive those packets, and that opens them up for MiTM attack where a malicious host can poison ARP caches of other hosts.

---

[15] https://bit.ly/2Cm5hPb

To prevent MiTM, a switch configured with DAI ensures that only valid ARP requests and responses are allowed. DAI figures out the validity of the ARP packet based on the valid MAC address to IP address bindings stored in a trusted database such as the DHCP snooping binding database.

Port Security

The port security feature allows you to restrict and secure communication on an L2 port by way of MAC address filtering. When you assign a secure MAC address to a port, the port will not forward any traffic that's not sourced from your allowed MAC address or addresses. By default, only one MAC address is allowed as a secure address.

If a port is configured as a secure port (**switchport port-security** command), and the maximum number of secure MAC addresses is reached, and if any newer MAC addresses are seen on the port i.e. the ones that are not already in the secure MAC address list then the switch will count that as a security violation event. You can configure the action that a switch will take for the port, also known as violation mode, in one of three ways.

1. Restrict mode
2. Protect mode
3. Shutdown mode (default)

You can pre-configure the port's behavior when a security violation takes place, something that's known as violation mode, which is an action that is being taken when a security violation is detected. You can configure the port to enter restrict mode, which restricts data from unsecure MAC addresses until a enough secure MAC addresses drop below the maximum value. When a port enters restrict mode, it also generates an SNMP trap. The protect mode behaves like restrict mode expect that there is no SNMP trap is generated.

If you do not configure any violation mode, the switch will use default shutdown mode. In shutdown mode, the port stops forwarding traffic altogether and enters a state known as error-disabled. You can bring the port out of this state by either entering a specific command (i.e., errdisable recovery cause psecure-violation) or by simply performing a shutdown and a no shut down.

Differentiate authentication, authorization, and accounting concepts

Authentication, Authorization, and Accounting (or AAA) is used by the network admins for controlling access to various network devices (such as FWs, routers, switches) as well as to authorize the commands that an admin can execute during the authenticated session. Command authorization is only supported by the TACACS+ protocol.

AAA is also used for access control by way of downloadable ACLs (or dACLs), which are Access Control Elements (or ACEs) that are downloaded after a session is authenticated and applied to the remote user session.

To enable authentication, authorization, and accounting (AAA) authentication for line logins, you can use the login authentication command in line configuration mode. You also need to configure AAA services.

Let's now configure user authentication via TACACS+.

```
router#configure terminal
Enter configuration commands, one per line.  End with CNTL/Z.
router(config)#aaa new-model
router(config)#aaa authentication login my-auth-list tacacs+
router(config)#tacacs-server host 192.168.1.101
router(config)#tacacs-server key cciein8weeks
router(config)#line 1 8
router(config-line)#login authentication my-auth-list
```

Describe wireless security protocols (WPA, WPA2, and WPA3)

The most common IEEE 802.11 Wi-Fi security protocols are Wired Equivalent Privacy (WEP), Wi-Fi Protected Access (WPA), WPA2, and WPA3.

WEP is the oldest and least secure Wi-Fi encryption, it is almost laughable to say the least. WPA is the evolution of WEP, but it is also woefully insecure. However, WPA2 did meet the primary goals of wireless security and is widely in use today.

WPA3 is the latest revision of WPA and provides in-transit security which allows use of AES-12 and AES-192 encryption. It also provides secure authentication but much like WPA2 still uses a pre-shared key to join a Wi-Fi network.

Configure WLAN using WPA2 PSK using the GUI

Traditionally, you configure a WLAN with PSK security, where all devices share the same PSK. Identity PSK is a feature that allows multiple PSKs, one for each client to be configured on the same SSID. When a client authenticates to a wireless network, WLC checks with a RADIUS server to if the MAC address exists in the auth policy. If it does, the RADIUS server will reply with an ACCESS-ACCEPT message, including PSK, as a Cisco-AVPair.

IPSK requires that you have either a Microsoft NPS (AD is a must) or use Cisco ISE, which makes it easier since client MACs can be assigned to Endpoint Identity Groups or EIGs and not have to be created as users.

For PSK configuration, you need to follow these steps.

- Log into WLC GUI
- Go to corresponding WLAN > Security > Layer 2 tab, and enable MAC Filtering.
- Now hop over to WLANs > Advanced Tabs and enable the "Allow AAA Override" option. You'll also need to select NAC State as "ISE NAC" if you are using the Cisco ISE server.

Chapter Summary

- The most common IEEE 802.11 Wi-Fi security protocols are Wired Equivalent Privacy (WEP), Wi-Fi Protected Access (WPA), WPA2, and WPA3.
- Authentication, Authorization, and Accounting (or AAA) is used by the network admins for controlling access to various network devices (such as FWs, routers, switches) as well as to authorize the commands that an admin can execute during the authenticated session
- The port security feature allows you to restrict and secure communication on an L2 port by way of MAC address filtering.
- Dynamic ARP Inspection (or DAI) is another L2 security feature that validates ARP packets. Each IP host maintains an ARP cache that contains IP to MAC bindings.
- DHCP snooping is an L2 security feature where a switch filters out untrusted DHCP messages based on a DHCP snooping binding table
- Access lists (or ACLs) are stateless L2-L4 packet filters to specify what should be permitted and denied inbound or outbound to and from a network.
- Password management complexity is a solution that helps manage rules you choose to implement password complexity within your enterprise
- There are two primary ways that you can use to configure the device access control, i.e. local username/passwords and remote Authentication, Authorization, and Accounting (or AAA) servers
- Malicious software (or the malware) is any software that was written with the malicious intent of damaging, stealing, or extorting
- Phishing attack uses social engineering methods such as duping a target into opening an email or a message such as WhatsApp or SMS

CHAPTER 6 AUTOMATION AND PROGRAMMABILITY

This chapter covers the following exam topics from Cisco's official 200-901 V1.0[16] Network Associate (CCNA) exam blueprint.

- Explain how automation impacts network management
- Compare traditional networks with controller-based networking
- Describe controller-based and software defined architectures (overlay, underlay, and fabric)
    - Separation of control plane and data plane
    - North-bound and south-bound APIs
- Compare traditional campus device management with Cisco DNA Center enabled device management
- Describe characteristics of REST-based APIs (CRUD, HTTP verbs, and data encoding)
- Recognize the capabilities of configuration management mechanisms Puppet, Chef, and Ansible
- Interpret JSON encoded data

---

[16] https://bit.ly/2PGgv4A

Explain how automation impacts network management

Historically, network devices have been configured in a device-by-device manner manually. While this worked well in smaller networks and before anything cloud-native was available, it doesn't work anymore. The growing network complexity, the ever-expanding DevOps/IaC software tooling ecosystem, simpler to use programming languages and APIs, most applications moving to the cloud and software-defined virtualized infrastructure, make a perfect case for making the leap towards network automation at scale. With automation, not only we can achieve better uptime but also drastically reduce network OPEX.

Following are among the few key use cases for applying network automation.

- Device provisioning (configuration management)
- Device software management (firmware management)
- Compliance (auditing networks)
- Reporting
- Troubleshooting (reactive and proactive)
- Data collection and streaming telemetry

Compare traditional networks with controller-based networking

While merchant silicon, from the likes of Broadcom, was around long before SDN, what SDN brought to the fore was clear separation of control and data plane in the form of a centralized network provisioning and management architecture that is controller-based with southbound and northbound APIs for integration with hardware and application software respectively.

In the process, SDN helped create software-based network overlays where many individual devices, physical or virtual, that could now be managed using a centralized controller as opposed to managing each device on its own with the help of an NMS.

	Controller-Based Model	**Device-Based Model**
Control Plane	Centralized	Distributed
Data Plane	Distributed	Distributed
Management Framework	Policy or intent-driven	NMS
Network Provisioning	API-driven automation	CLIs, GUIs etc.
Network Monitoring	Streamed Telemetry (publisher/subscriber)	NMS/SNMP
AI/ML-based Operations	Yes	No

Controller-based management can fully take advantage of software-driven innovation esp. AI and ML in the areas of provisioning, monitoring, and operations. As we speak, all networking vendors are prioritizing API interfaces for newer features over implementing newer CLIs or GUIs.

Describe controller-based and software defined architectures (overlay, underlay, and fabric)

The concept of overlays, i.e. virtual topology built on top of a physical network, started with SDN and DC networking. However, with the advent of SD-WAN, the overlays made their way into WAN.

For DC networks, Virtual Extensible VLAN (or VXLAN) is used to create virtual overlays on top of a physical underlay. VXLAN uses MAC in IP/UDP tunneling to extend L2 segments over IP networks. VXLAN uses flood and learn mechanisms much like ethernet itself. Ethernet VPNs (or EVPNs) is a variation where VXLANs are used along with BGP to accomplish routing between endpoints.

Cisco SD-WAN components and their actual functions within the SD-WAN fabric, let us now compare the two solutions, i.e. age-old traditional WAN versus SD-WAN.

	Traditional WAN	**SD-WAN**
Bandwidth cost	Expensive private or	Performant WAN

	MPLS circuits	overlay built on top of a variety of WAN underlay transports
DC dependency	No direct access to cloud apps due to age-old hair pinned or backhauled hub/spoke design in order to meet centralized policy enforcement requirement	Enterprise-grade performance for both cloud and DC bound traffic
Complexity	Complex to manage due to mostly single-function appliances and routers,	Easier to manage, and PAYG model
Application Performance	Application performance is unpredictable due to several point devices not centrally controlled or managed	Application performant branch, due to the clear separation of routing from the service insertion on-prem, cloud or in the DC

Cisco SD-WAN virtual IP fabric transforms a complex legacy network into an easy-to-manage, scalable network in five steps:
1. Separate transport from the service side of the network.
2. Centralize routing intelligence and enable segmentation.
3. Secure the network automatically.
4. Influence reachability through centralized policy.
5. Simplify orchestration and provisioning.

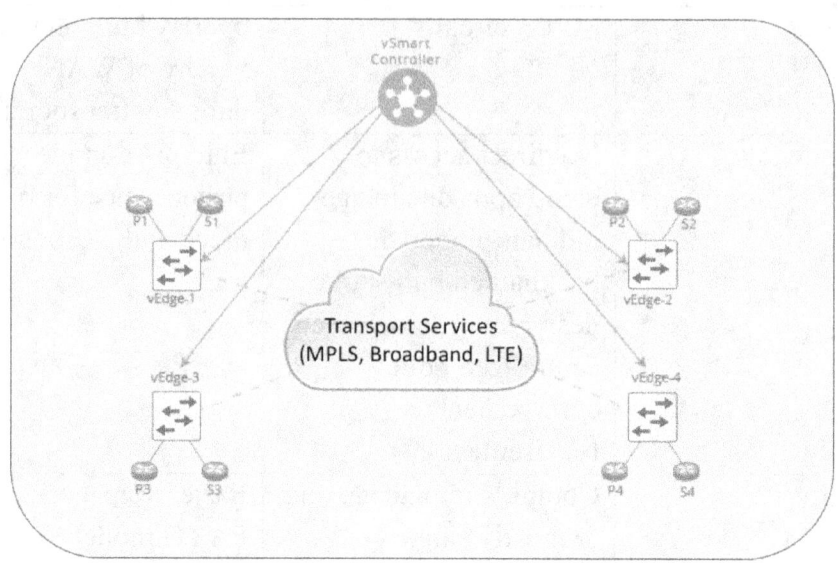

vEdge devices and vSmart controller connect via a TLS based control plane. You can configure certificates within vManage for encrypted and authenticated communication. Each vEdge device can send traffic directly to another without exchanging any reachability information. To provide scale, the SD-WAN solution uses IEEE's Overlay Management Protocol (or OMP) that carries QoS, routing policy, multicast and IPSec keys.

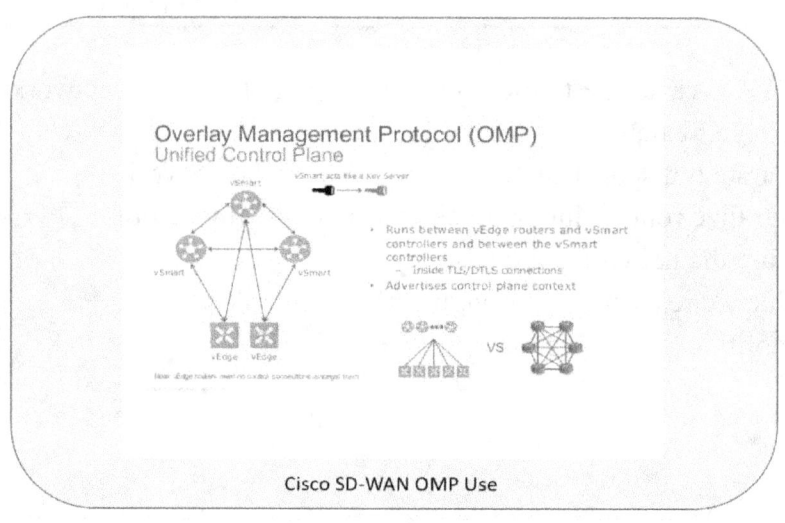

Cisco SD-WAN OMP Use

Cisco SD-WAN solution supports IPSec ESP and GRE encapsulations for its overlay network. There is no IKE needed since the key exchange is handled by OMP. Absence of IKE helps speed up vEdge to vEdge tunnel setup time. The solution can classify traffic based on ports, protocols, IP addresses, and IP DSCP values. It can also classify traffic based on applications. Policies are configured via vManage dashboard, and once done, are communicated to vSmart controller, which in turn communicates them to vEdge devices. If a vSmart controller goes down, affected vEdge devices can continue with the last known good configuration.

Zero-touch provisioning relies on vBond which allows vEdge devices to connect into vSmart controller without any prior configuration. Each vEdge device contains an SSL certificate. All vEdge devices must be trusted by the vManage before they can be managed by the vSmart controller.

For brownfield deployment, the solution allows integration with VRF/VLAN by using a 4-byte shim header known as the label, which is part of each packet in the overlay and functions as sort of a membership ID.

Here are the resources requirements for vBond, vEdge, vManage, and vSmart Controller components. Please note that vBond, vManage, and vSmart Controller requirements depend on the vEdge devices that are needed to be provisioned.

Cisco provides complete hardware and software installation guidelines and requirements[17].

1-50 Devices	vBond Orchestrator	vEdge	vManage	vSmart Controller
vCPUs	2	2	16	2
vRAM (GB)	4	2	32	4
SSD (GB)	10	10	20	16

---

[17] https://bit.ly/31eQSwP

Bandwidth (Mbps)	1	Up to 2	25	2
Hypervisor	ESXi / KVM			

Further Reading
SD-WAN Cloud Scale Architecture[18]

Separation of control plane and data plane

You can divide a networking device into four distinct logical groups as far as traffic to/from or through a device is concerned.

1. Data plane (traffic that is not sourced or destined from/to the device, i.e., transit traffic)
2. The control plane (traffic sourced or destined from/to the device, traffic type used for the creation and operation of the network such as BGP, OSPF, and ARP)
3. Management plane (technically same as control plane traffic but for network management such as TFTP, SSH, SNMP, FTP, NTP, etc.)
4. Services plane (a case of data plane traffic but in this case, router is involved in modifying the packet header or payload, such as GRE, QoS, NAT, etc.)

---

[18] https://bit.ly/2vAp4XM

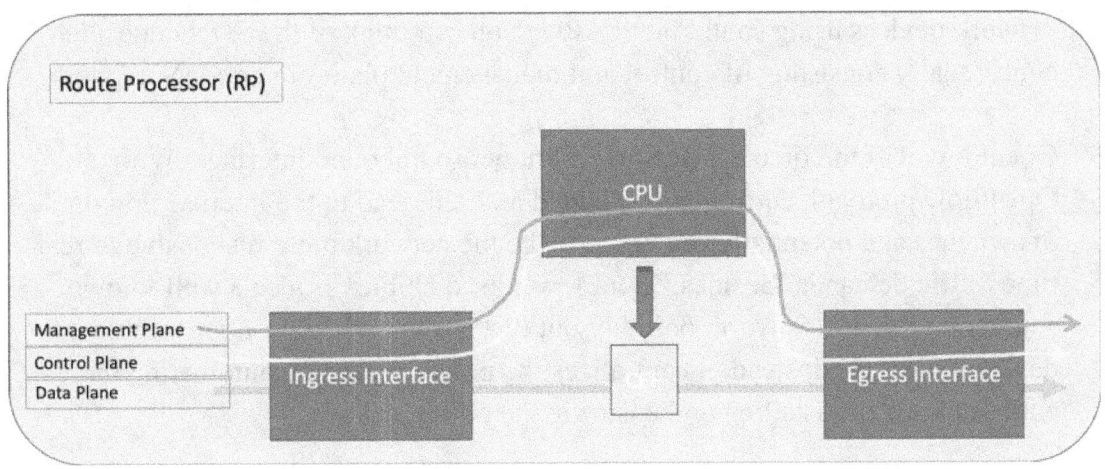

SDN is about network programmability based on disaggregation and as per Cisco, there are four different types of SDN models out there.

- The distributed control plane model outlines how things were before SDN came along. Before SDN, each router or switch relies on its control plane information to make routing and forwarding decisions.
- The augmented control plane model uses a centralized controller that can apply a policy by injecting IP prefixes, PBR, or ACLs objects. This model represents an incremental change from the distributed control plane model, or shall we call it pre-SDN status quo. PfR controller is an example of an augmented control plane model.
- The hybrid control plane model, which is an extension of the augmented model except for that controller, is now able to control the entire network as opposed to just the "parts." Cisco APIC is an example of such a model in which failure of the centralized controller causes end devices to use their control plane intelligence.
- A centralized control plane model is what most of relating with the SDN, i.e., a single controller controls the entire topology and directly manipulates the forwarding decision making or data plane.

Southbound APIs facilitate efficient control over the network infrastructure and enable the SDN controller to make changes to the device's data plane dynamically. SDN controller is the central process that communicates with network devices using southbound APIs. You can think of the SDN controller conceptually consisting of control and management planes in an SDN network.

OpenFlow was the first and most well-known southbound interface. With OpenFlow protocol, entries can be added and removed to the internal flow-table of switches and potentially routers to make the network more responsive to real-time traffic demands. Besides OpenFlow, Cisco OpFlex is also a well-known southbound API. It is worth pointing out that Cisco APIC doesn't manipulate the data path directly; instead, it centralizes the policy definition automating the entire process of installing and ensuring the policy.

More established networking protocols have also found their ways to run in an SDN environment as southbound protocols, such as BGP-LS and PCEP. BGP-LS is a southbound protocol that can be used to export IGP information from the network to the SDN controller. BGP-LS is an extension to BGP for distributing the network's link-state (LS) topology model to external entities.

OpenDaylight (ODL) is an open source and modular SDN controller for customizing and automating networks of any size and scale. Cisco Open SDN controller supports OVSDB, OpenFlow, BGP-LS, NETCONF, and PCEP as southbound protocols. It represents hardened, validated, and supported OpenDaylight distribution. OpenContrail and ONOS are also examples of SDN controllers, geared more for carrier-grade environments.

OpFlex was designed to augment rather than replace tools (such as OVSDB) by focusing on additional requirements of the network and policies that must span multiple network devices. It includes a native mechanism for identity resolution used to define declarative policies between two different network endpoints. It is an open and extensible policy protocol for transferring abstract policy in XML or JSON between a network policy controller such as the Cisco APIC and any device, including hypervisor switches, physical switches, and Layer 4 through 7 network services.

Northbound APIs are the most critical APIs in the SDN environment since the value of SDN is also tied to the innovative applications it can potentially support and enable. Northbound APIs utilize REST APIs.

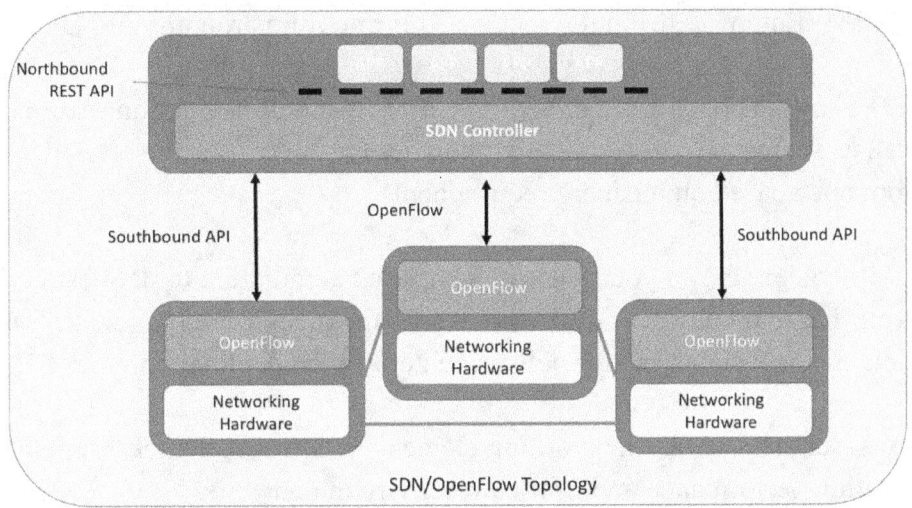

Compare traditional campus device management with Cisco DNA Center enabled device management

Cisco DNA Center is at the center of Cisco's intent-based networking initiative. Cisco customers and partners can use APIs, integration flows, events and notification services and Cisco DNA Center SDK to create applications above and beyond the features it natively provides.

It is a controller as well as an analytics platform that makes Cisco's intent-based networking possible. It consists of five major components.

- Design
- Policy
- Provision
- Assurance
- Platform

DNA Center Dashboard

DNA Design component allows you to design your network using workflows while allowing for importing existing network designs and device images from APIC-EM (Enterprise Module) and Cisco Prime Infrastructure into DNA Center.

DNA Policy is about user and device profiles that help deliver on secure access as well as segmentation. Application policies ensure consistent network performance based on business requirements.

DNA Provision allows you to use policy-based automation to deliver services to network-based on business priority and simplifies device deployment. It is the module that is responsible for delivering zero-touch deployment.

DNA Assurance enables networking elements to stream telemetry for ensuring application performance and user connectivity in real-time.

DNA Platform allows developers to directly access the DNA through the developer toolkit or SDK. To review APIs, you can click on Platform > Developer Toolkit.

DNA center appliance hosts SDN controller, analytics engine and telemetry storage. At the time of writing, a 44-core DNA appliance (DN2-HW-APL) is listed for USD 88.6K in Cisco's GPL. It must be installed and run on the bundled bare metal server, as we speak, there is no virtual appliance package available.

DNA center licenses come in three flavors, i.e.

- Essentials (includes basic automation and network visibility)
- Advantage (includes Essentials, plus advanced automation, image lifecycle management, AI/ML analytics and assurance and API/SDK integration)
- Premier (Everything in Advantage, plus encrypted traffic analytics and multi-domain policy segmentation)

Let's now look at the various aspects of DNA dashboard and types of data it provides.

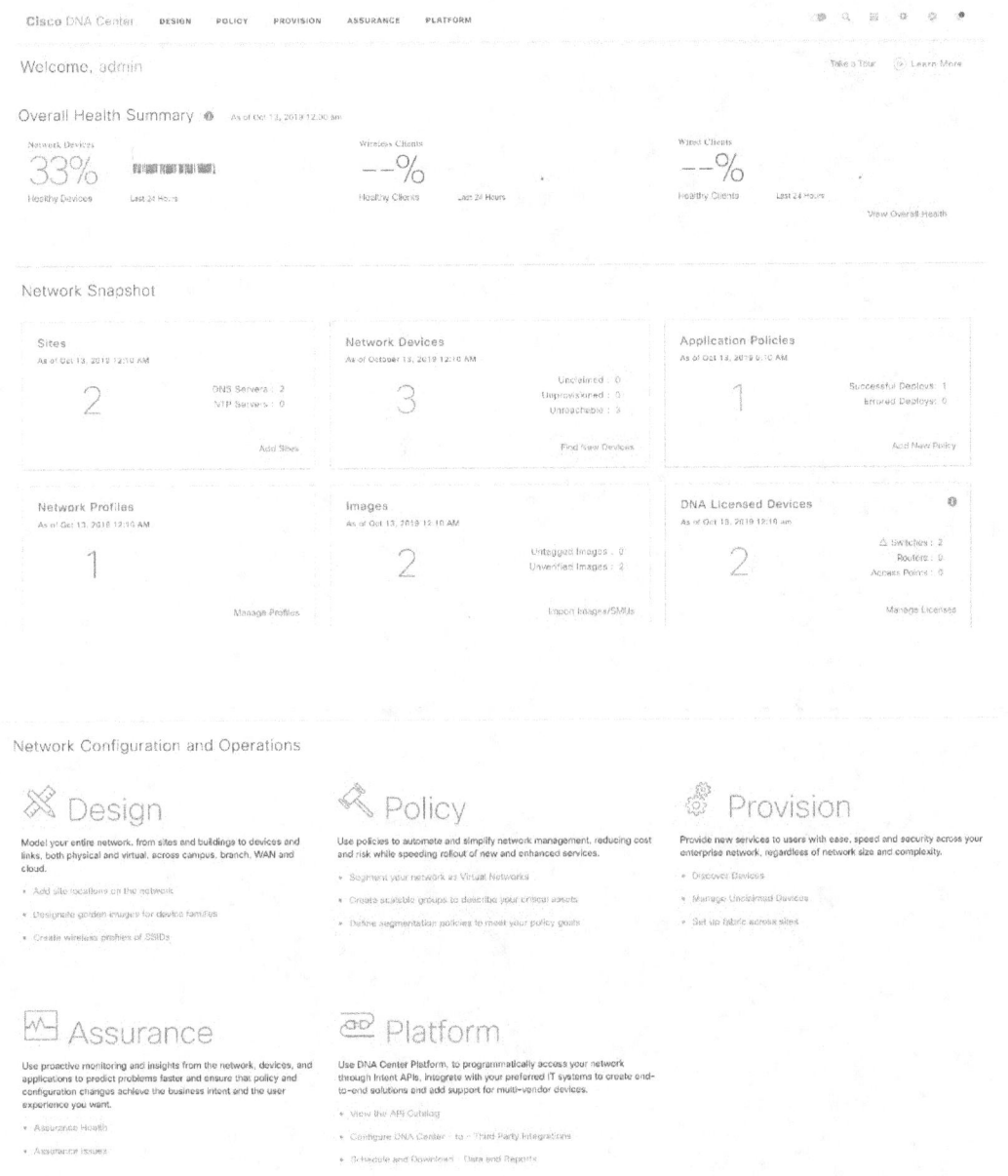

Tools

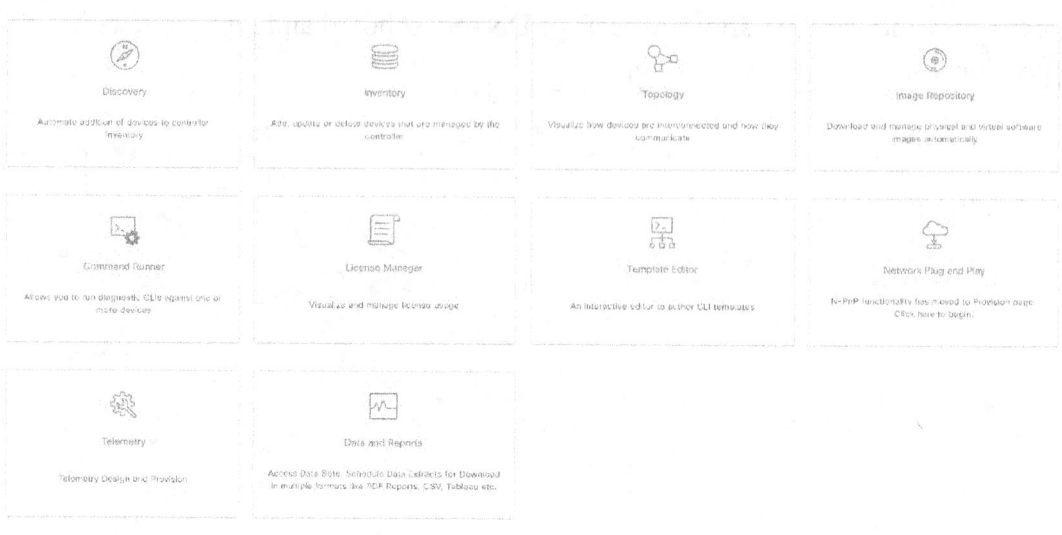

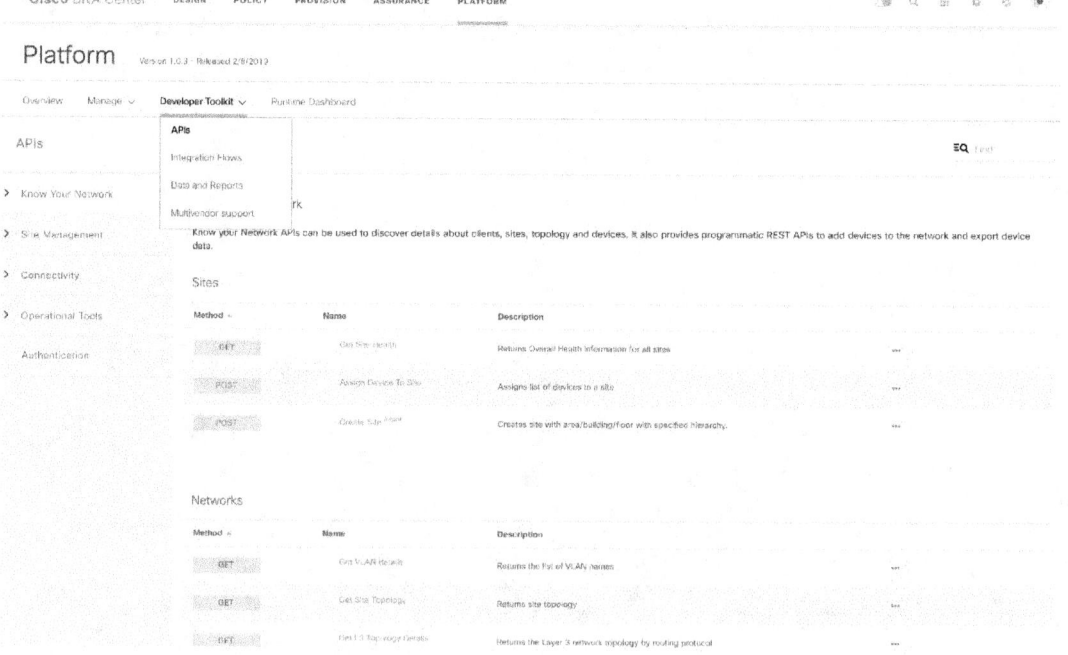

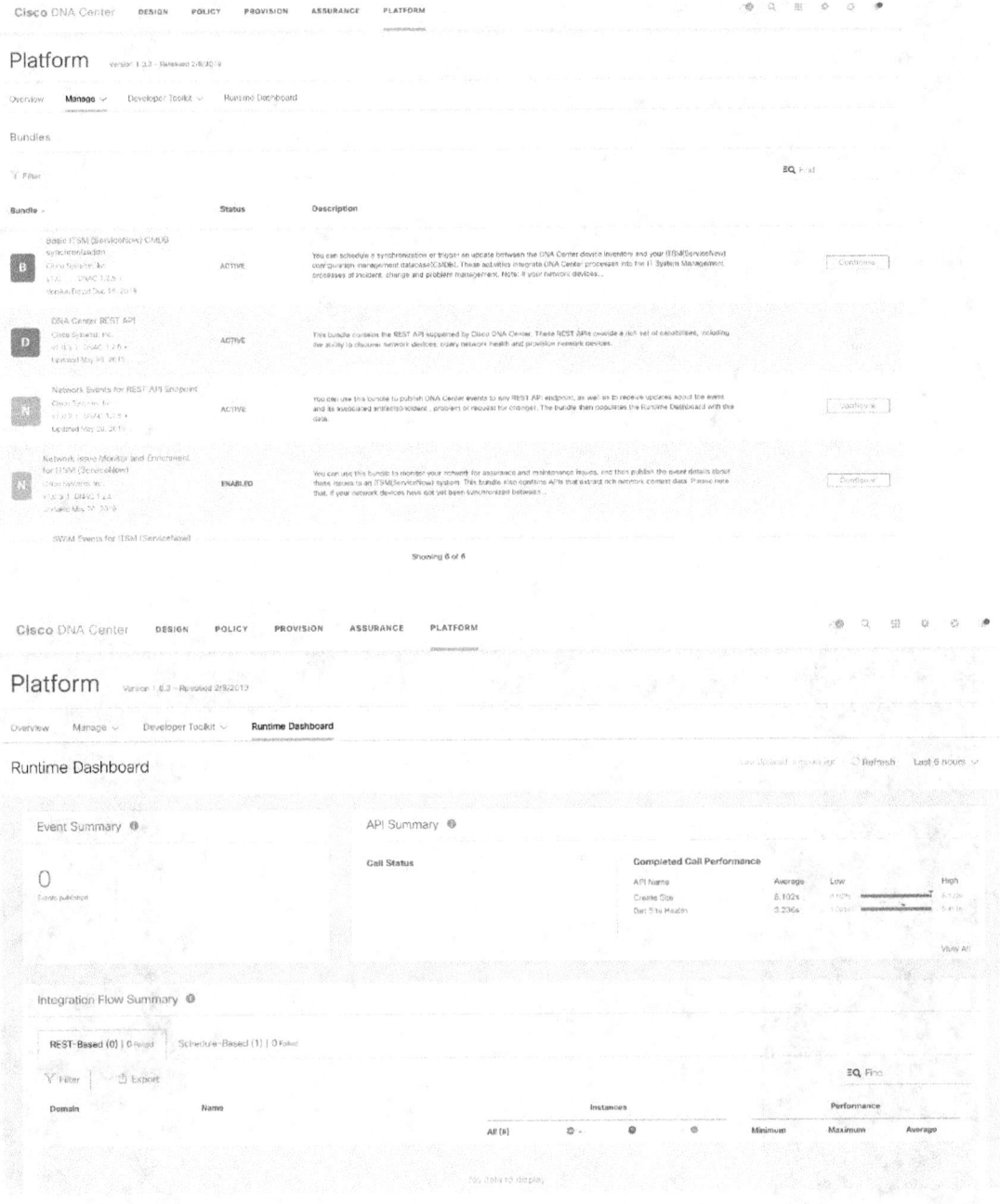

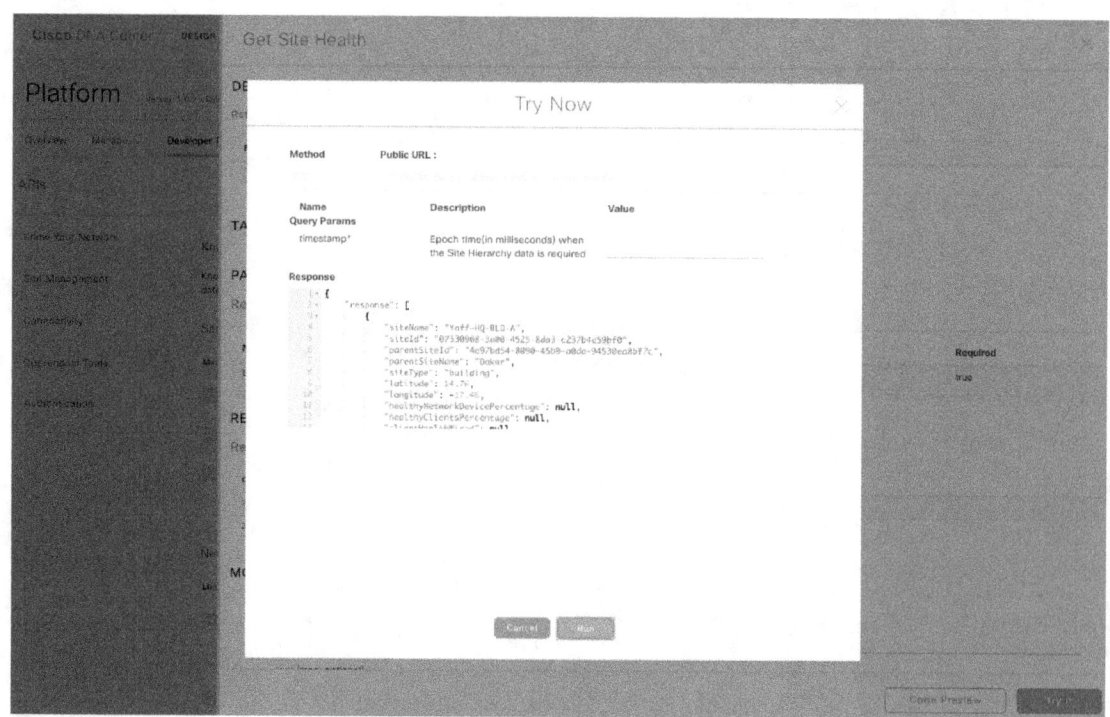

Toolkit provides information about all the API calls that are part of the SDK. However, before we proceed further, let's summarize the types of APIs that are available with the DNA Center.

- Northbound APIs
- Southbound APIs
- Eastbound APIs
- Westbound APIs

Northbound APIs, also known as, Intent APIs provide support for policy-based abstraction of business intent, allowing focus on business outcomes as opposed to mechanics of how. It is a RESTful APIs that allows the use of GET, POST, PUT and DELETE HTTP methods with JSON encoding to discover and control the network. All API calls require the use of a security token that identifies the privileges of an authenticated user making the RESTful API calls. You must obtain a security token before you can make use of any of the DNA center APIs.

177

Southbound APIs allow managing non-Cisco infrastructure by way of SDK that allow the creation of packages for 3rd party devices. Package contains mapping of Cisco DNA center features to other vendors' southbound protocols. In summary, southbound APIs are a gateway to multivendor support within the Cisco DNA center.

Events and Notifications provide the ability to establish a notification handler, so when specific DNA center events are triggered, such as SoftWare Image Management (SWIM) events, 3rd party systems can take actions in response to those events. Notifications can also be generated for internal events such as Assurance event causing an external ITSM system to initiate a ticket.

Westbound APIs, or what's also known as Integration APIs, are provided so that other 3rd party systems such as ITSM can be integrated with Cisco DNA center. Using integration APIs, you can implement change management, and approval and pre-approval chains. They also allow integration for reporting and analytics capabilities such as capacity planning, asset management, compliance control, and auditing. Finally, integration APIs allow support for IT4IT reference architecture so if you are using an external system that supports that, you can be sure to optimize your end to end IT value chain.

Further Reading
Cisco DNA Center User Guides[19]
Cisco DNA Center Maintain and Operate Guides[20]
Cisco DNA Center Install and Upgrade Guides[21]

Describe characteristics of REST-based APIs (CRUD, HTTP verbs, and data encoding)

---

[19] https://bit.ly/2w2rWNH

[20] https://bit.ly/2TLz7mB

[21] https://bit.ly/3cOxpbA

Representational State Transfer (or REST) was described by Roy Fielding in 2000 as part of his PhD dissertation. He described six constraints or principles for REST (not to be confused with REST APIs!). These constraints can be applied to any protocol and when that happens, it is known as RESTful.

- Client/server
- Stateless
- Cache
- Uniform interface
- Layered system
- Code-on-demand

Let's understand each of those constraints one by one.

The client and the server should be independent of each other, e.g. where one client can be built for multiple server platforms. Client/server refers to the assumption that clients and server applications MUST be able to evolve and develop independently, a client only needs to know the resource URIs.

The requests from the client to server must be standalone, i.e. there is no concept of a session. The server cannot contain session states. Make all client/server interaction stateless, but why? Because if you make a client app stateful, then it needs to communicate the entire lifecycle of user states to the remote server which isn't good for the server as a client should simply store the user states while no context is stored or preserved between REST requests.

The server dictates if the response is cacheable or not, if it is cacheable then client can use the data from the response for another request later on. Caching can be implemented on the client or server-side, and it is hugely useful for performance reasons including minimizing some client/server communication. The uniform interface, i.e. the interface between the client and the server, is based on four principles of its own.

- Identification of resources
- Manipulation of resources through representations
- Self-descriptive messages
- Hypermedia as the engine of application state

The system is made up of different layers and where each layer under provides services only to the layer above it (much like what happens in case of OSI stack). REST allows the use of layered system architecture, i.e. a web server where APIs are hosted may store its database on another server and authentication information on yet another one without exposing any of this to the client.

Lastly, the code-on-demand is an optional constraint and simply describes the fact that information returned by a REST service can include executable code, or link to code, etc. Code-on-demand is used by payment gateways such as Stripe, where they send in a JavaScript file that is downloaded and executed by the client. There is no doubt that if used without security measures, code-on-demand can become a security risk.

REST web service API or REST API is a programming interface that adheres to the principles of REST and communicates over HTTP. REST APIs use the following components of the HTTP.

- HTTP requests/responses
- HTTP verbs or methods
- HTTP status codes
- HTTP headers/body

There are four major components of a REST API call.

- Uniform Resource Identifier (URI)
- HTTP method
- Header
- Body

The URI or URL identifies which resource the client wants to manipulate. The URI syntax consists of the following components:

- Scheme
- Authority
- Path
- Query

With all the four pieces together, it looks like the following.

scheme:[//authority][/path][?query]

or

https://fullstacknetworker.com:443/v1/products/?q=DevNetAssociate

The scheme refers to the transport protocol, for REST APIs, there are only two choices, HTTP or HTTPS (HTTP with TLS). The authority or destination consist of two parts, the host and port. The path, also known as resource path, simply represents the location of the resource, or data or an object. The query and the parameter are optional. If a query is present, it is preceded by a question mark (?) as shown in the example above.

Further Reading
Getting Started with APIs[22]

HTTP Method	Action (CRUD)
POST	Create (C)
GET	Retrieve (R)
PUT	Update (U), existing resource
PATCH	Update (U), partial update on a resource
DELETE	Delete (D)

[22] https://bit.ly/2TVkn3o

In summary, the HTTP response or status code means the following.

- 1XX: Informational (e.g. 101 means Switching Protocols)
- 2XX: Success (e.g. 200 means OK)
- 3XX: Redirection (e.g. 301 means Moved Permanently)
- 4XX: Client Error (e.g. 401 Unauthorized, 403 Forbidden, 404 Not Found etc.)
- 5XX: Server Error (e.g. 500 Internal Server Error, 502 Bad Gateway, 503 Service Unavailable etc.)

Now, let's look at some of the specific response codes and their description.

HTTP Response Code	Status Message	Description
200	OK	Good
201	Created	New resource created
400	Bad Request	Invalid request
401	Unauthorized	Missing/Incorrect authentication
403	Forbidden	Not allowed
404	Not Found	Resource not found
500	Internal Server Error	Something wrong with the server
503	Service Unavailable	Server is unable to complete request
504	Gateway Timeout	Server timeout

Recognize the capabilities of configuration management mechanisms Puppet, Chef, and Ansible

Before we discuss the automation tools, it is crucial to revisit some of the core concepts related to automation.

182

Idempotency is about producing desired results each time an automation is run. It enables convergence and composability. It enables you to both gather collections and deploy collections to perform incremental upgrades. For example, if you have a Docker cluster and there is a misconfiguration, you can roll back the most recent change and then rebuild the entire cluster.

As we discussed earlier, procedural code can achieve idempotency but most of the infrastructure automation tools use declarative or static model that represents the desired outcome. Ansible and Puppet use declarative Domain-Specific Languages (or DSLs), whereas Chef uses procedural approach to infrastructure automation.

It is also important to understand the various operations terms such as provisioning, configuration, deployment and orchestration.

Provisioning means obtaining a resource, enabling communications and putting it into service. For example, installing an operating system. It is generally about the lower-level platform readiness. Configuration means installing applications and services on top of the lower-level platform that has already been provisioned. Deployment is about building, arranging and integrating applications such as database or Kubernetes clusters often across multiple nodes. Orchestration has to do with managing workload and lifecycles and reacting to changes in real-time such as autoscaling. In the abstract form, it refers to workflow automation that carries out tasks to deliver business results.

Ansible is an open source automation tool or platform that is easy to setup and can help you with the following tasks.

- Configuration management
- Application deployment
- Task automation or Orchestration

Ansible architecture is simple and lightweight.

- Control node (can run on any Linux machine that has Python installed). It connects to managed devices using SSH to execute shell commands, inject Python scripts, etc.
- Plugins enable Ansible to gather facts from and perform operations on infrastructure that doesn't support running Python locally.

Ansible folder hierarchy includes the following components.

- Inventory files (or hostfiles help organize inventory of resources)
- Variable files (files that describe the variables values related to groups of hosts and individual hosts)
- Library and utility files (Python code for custom modules and utilities)
- Main playbook files (YAML files)
- Role folders and files (role folder that contains a /tasks folder and main.yaml tasks file)

Configuration management tools include Ansible, Puppet, and Chef and they are well known in the DevOps circles. These tools enable you to automate applications, infrastructure, and networks to a high degree without the need to do any manual programming. Puppet is written in Ruby and refers to its automation instruction set as Puppet manifests. The major point to note here is that Puppet is agent-based. Agent-based means a software agent needs to be installed on all devices you want to manage with Puppet. "Devices" here refers to servers, routers, switches, firewalls, and the like. It is often not possible to load an agent on many networking devices. Hence, this requirement limits the number of devices that can be used with Puppet out of the box. The agent requirement raises the barriers to deployment for Puppet as far as networking is concerned. Furthermore, with some investment and cultural change, DevOps virtuous cycle brings with it the benefits of improved scalability, reliability, maintainability, and faster release rollouts with higher quality.

Chef, another popular configuration management tool, follows much of the same model as Puppet. Chef is written in Ruby and uses a declarative model, is also agent-based. Chef refers to its automation instruction as recipes and when they are grouped, they are known as cookbooks.

The two notable differences between Puppet, Chef, and Ansible are that Ansible is written in Python and that it is natively agentless. Being agentless significantly lowers the barrier to deployment from an automation perspective.

Ansible can integrate and automate any device using any API. For example, integrations can use REST APIs, NETCONF, SSH, or even SNMP, if desired. Ansible sets of tasks (instructions) are known as playbooks. Each playbook is made up of one or more plays, where each play consists of individual tasks.

	Chef	**Puppet**	**Ansible**
Who owns it	Chef Labs	Puppet Labs	Red Hat
Agent	Required	Required	Not Required
Language written in	Ruby	Ruby	Python
Tasks are known as	recipes	manifests	plays
Group of tasks known as	cookbooks	modules	playbooks
Config Language	Custom	Custom	YAML
Ease of Use	Steep learning curve	Steep learning curve with DSL/Ruby	Easier
Pricing	Free (Chef Basics), $72/node	Free (Open Source) up to 10 nodes,	Free (CLI), unlimited nodes

		afterwards	$120/node afterwards	Free (Ansible Tower) up to 10 nodes, paid afterwards with or without support. Tower pricing ranges from $50-$175 per managed node per year. Ansible Engine and Tower provide essentially same functionalities except that the Engine comes with the CLI whereas Tower is web-based.

When using the configuration management tools, from a RESTful service standpoint, for an operation (or service call) to be idempotent, clients can make that same call repeatedly while producing the same result.

Puppet comprises of a little more complex architecture than Ansible. It consists of the following components.

- Designated server to host main application components such as puppet server (formerly puppet master), facter, and puppetDB. It can run on a VM or a container. Puppet server requires a Network Time Protocol (NTP) client.
- Secure client (Puppet agent, it needs to be installed and configured on the target devices)
- Puppet modules (for targets that can't run Puppet agent)

Puppet is heavier than Ansible and thus requires more hardware resource to run. Like Ansible, Puppet provides a host of resources that can be executed to define configuration actions to be performed on target hosts. A single Puppet server can manage up to 4,000 hosts. You can find plenty of Puppet modules for Cisco ISO and Cisco UCS (via UCSM).

Chef provides a complete system for working with IaC. There are there main Chef components.

- Chef workstation (standalone operator workstation)
- Chef Infra client (the host agent, it runs on hosts and retrieve configuration templates. Cookbooks enable control of hardware devices such as Cisco routers and switches since you can't run Chef client locally)
- Chef Infra server (It replies to queries from Chef infra agents on validated hosts and responds with configuration updates, etc.)

Cisco provides modified Chef Infra agents that run in the guest shell of NX-OS. Cisco also maintains Chef Cookbook for NX-OS infrastructure. Cisco UCS infrastructure is easily managed with Chef via a cookbook that enables integration with Cisco IMC (via UCSM). You can also integrate with Intersight via Python or PowerShell SDKs.

NSO and Ansible can be used integrated. Ansible tasks use modules (as Clients) to perform their activities whereas NSO uses JSON RPC API perform operations on NSO. NSO can use YANG modules to describe the schema of the data can be modified using JSON RPC.

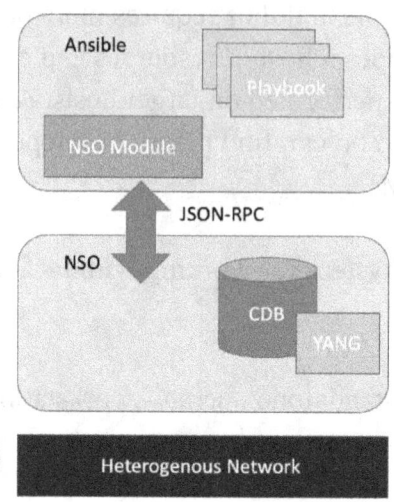

Interpret JSON, XML and YAML encoded data

When using Application Programming Interfaces (or APIs) through software, it is super critical to receive and transmit data in forms that are standards-based and machine and human readable.

Let's go over a few reasons why it is so.

- It allows use of off-the-shelf software tools to convert and accept them into native data structures (e.g. JSON value/pairs to Python dictionaries)
- It makes it easier to write code that communicates with messages in format that another remote endpoint can easily consume
- It is easier to read and manipulate received messages
- It makes it easier to detect malformed messages

Extensible Markup Language (XML) and JavaScript Object Notation (or JSON, pronounced as Jay-sun) and YAML Ain't Markup Language (YAML) are the main data encoding formats used in remote APIs today. JSON is both a human-friendly and machine-readable format and sends data in name-value pairs.

JSON and YAML can be converted to each other without much effort. JSON is best known for the curly brace syntax. It is popular because it is easier to read and natively maps to Python dictionary data structure. However, XML is bit of an outlier, it is less simple to parse and convert to JSON or YAML. It is an older format so there are plenty of mature APIs that still use it.

Parsing JSON, YAML and XML is a common requirement of interacting with REST APIs.

XML Example

XML is the parent of HTML. It is generic method to wrapping textual data in symmetrical tags to indicate semantics. XML files typically carry an extension of .xml.

```xml
<?xml version="1.0" encoding="utf-8"?>
<root>
 <persons>
  <element>
   <gender>male</gender>
   <name>Jeff Bezos</name>
  </element>
  <element>
   <gender>male</gender>
   <name>Elon Musk</name>
  </element>
  <element>
   <gender>female</gender>
```

```
        <name>Jessica Alba</name>
    </element>
  </persons>
</root>
```

XML Prologue

The first line in XML file is known as the XML prologue. It has a special format and bracketed by <? and ?>. It contains the tag name xml and attributes stating the version and a character encoding. Normally, you'd find the version to be "1.0" and the character encoding to be "UTF-8" or 8-bit Unicode Transformation Format.

XML Comments

XML files can include comments, much like their HTML counterpart, they are enclosed in <! -- and --> tags.

XML Body

Everything after the prologue is the XML body. The individual elements are surrounded by symmetrical pairs of tags, the opening tag < and the closing tag > symbols. The closing tag includes a "/" preceding the closing tag.

The main body of the document is always surrounded by an outermost tag pair, e.g. <root> and </root> in the example.

The structure of an XML document is like a tree with branches (known as elements) containing further branches (known as sub-elements), e.g. <element></element> are elements whereas <gender></gender> are sub-elements.

```
<persons>
    <element>
        <gender>male</gender>
        <name>Jeff Bezos</name>
    </element>
    <element>
        <gender>male</gender>
        <name>Elon Musk</name>
    </element>
    <element>
        <gender>female</gender>
        <name>Jessica Alba</name>
    </element>
</persons>
```

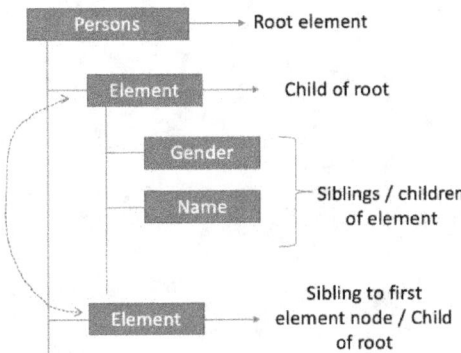

XML Attributes

XML allows you to embed attributes inside the tags to convey additional information. Version and the encoding types in the XML prologue are examples of attributes. Attribute values are carried inside double quotes and an element can have multiple attributes each with a unique name.

XML Namespaces

Some XML messages or documents incorporate a reference to a specific namespace to convey how they should be consumed. Namespaces are defined by standard bodies such as the IETF, e.g. xml:ns:netconf for NETCONF.

JSON Example

Now, let's convert above XML into JSON.

```
{
  "persons": [
    {
      "name": "Jeff Bezos",
```

```
    "gender": "male"
  },
  {
    "name": "Elon Musk",
    "gender": "male"
  },
  {
    "name": "Jessica Alba",
    "gender": "female"
  }
 ]
}
```

JSON Data Types

JSON data types include numbers, strings, and boolean (True or False). JSON filenames typically end in ".json".

JSON Objects

Much like JavaScript, individual objects comprise of key/value pairs surrounded by braces e.g. {"key":"value"}.

JSON Maps and Lists

Objects can also contain multiple key/value pairs, separated by commas, like Python dictionaries. JSON values can also contain lists of data objects.

Unlike XML or YAML, JSON doesn't support adding any kind of comments. JSON format also doesn't give any significance to whitespaces, so you can ident your JSON data using tabs or spaces or nothing at all.

YAML Example

YAML format is like a superset of JSON but even easier to read. One of the most commonly known use of YAML is configuration files and particularly for writing declarative automation templates such as Ansible playbooks. YAML parsers can also parse JSON but not vice versa.

YAML File Structure

YAML files open with "---" and end with "…". You can also have multiple YAML documents within one file where each document is separated by "---". YAML filenames typically end in ".yaml".

YAML Data Types

YAML data types include numbers, strings, and Booleans. Strings don't need to be quoted, quotes are only needed when strings contain characters that have meaning in YAML.

YAML Indentation and File Structure

YAML uses indentation to describe hierarchies. Items indented below a label are considered members of that labeled element. There are no specific requirements for indentation amount, you can use a space or a tab. However, the best practice is to use two spaces per indent level.

YAML Maps and Lists

YAML maps can contain multiple key/value pairs and ordered lists. Maps are expresses over multiple lines, beginning with a label key and a colon, followed by members.

```
1  this-is-a-map:
2      key: 5
3      anotherkey: Full Stack Networker
```

Lists are represented in a similar way, but members are preceded with a hyphen (dash) and a space.

```
1  this-is-a-list:
2  - 1
3  - 2
4  - 3
5  - 5
```

Maps and lists can also be written in flow syntax (much like Python).

```
1  this-is-a-map: { key: 5, anotherkey: Full Stack Networker}
2  this-is-a-list: [1, 2, 3, 5]
```

YAML Comments

Comments in YAML can be inserted anywhere inside the document except for in a long string. All comments are preceded by the hash sign.

```
1  # YAML is fun
2  this-is-a-map: { key: 5, anotherkey: Full Stack Networker}
3  this-is-a-list: [1, 2, 3, 5]
```

Now, let's convert our JSON document into YAML.

```
persons:
    -
        name: 'Jeff Bezos'
        gender: male
    -
        name: 'Elon Musk'
        gender: male
    -
        name: 'Jessica Alba'
        gender: female
```

As we discussed earlier, XML is a markup language much like HTML and consists of a set of rules for encoding documents that are human and machine-readable. XML was formally defined in W3C specifications. Using XML, you can define your tags or elements, their order, and how they are supposed to be processed or displayed on screen. XML encoded file can live on a server or take on a transient when being transmitted between two machines.

One of the most distinguishing characteristics of XML is that it allows you to define your tags or elements, as opposed to HTML where tags are standardized. It is like HTML, but at the same time more flexible, i.e. it is both a language as well as a meta-language where you can define other languages using as it the basis, for example, RSS or XSLT.

XML Parsing in Python

Parsing means analyzing a message and breaking it into its components. When messages are transmitted over the wire, they are communicated as a stream of characters. Upon arrival, they need to be parsed into a semantically appropriate data structure where each component is recognized as an integer, float, string, and so on.

Compiling source code is also a type of parsing. Serialization, on the other hand, is about converting a data structure into a format that can be transmitted. When you use a REST API which reads data from Python dictionaries and output them as equivalent JSON/YAML/XML in string form to the remote resource – when you are serializing, you are encoding. Deserialization is a parsing (or decoding); it takes serialized data and recreates the original data structure from it.

Python allows you to parse, modify and build XML documents. Your XML document can be stored in a file or the form of a string. There are two well-known methods to parse XML with Python, i.e. you can use the ElementTree (ET) APIs or the Minidom module to load and parse XML.

The XML data format is hierarchical and the most fitting way to represent that data is with a tree. ET has two classes to help break that hierarchy down into two levels, i.e. ElementTree which represents the whole XML document as a tree and Element which represents a single node in that tree.

Interaction with the entire document, such as reading and writing files, is commonly done using the ElementTree, whereas interactions with a single XML element (or child) or sub-elements (or sub-child) are carried out using the Element level.

Using the ElementTree APIs to parse XML

XML Document

```
<persons>
 <element>
  <gender>male</gender>
  <name>Jeff Bezos</name>
 </element>
 <element>
  <gender>male</gender>
  <name>Elon Musk</name>
 </element>
 <element>
```

```
    <gender>female</gender>
    <name>Jessica Alba</name>
  </element>
</persons>
```

Python Code

```python
1  import xml.etree.ElementTree as ET
2  tree = ET.parse('persons.xml')
3  root = tree.getroot()
4
5  print(ET.tostring(root, encoding = 'utf8').decode('utf8'))
6
7  print('\nNumber of Elements:')
8  print(len(root))
9  print('\nNumber of Sub-Elements:')
10 print(len(root[0]))
11
12 print('\nElem/Sub-Elem Data:')
13 for elem in root:
14     for subelem in elem:
15         print(subelem.tag + ":" + subelem.text)
```

Code Output

```
<?xml version='1.0' encoding='utf8'?>
<persons>
        <element>
                <gender>male</gender>
                <name>Jeff Bezos</name>
        </element>
        <element>
                <gender>male</gender>
                <name>Elon Musk</name>
        </element>
        <element>
                <gender>female</gender>
                <name>Jessica Alba</name>
        </element>
</persons>

Number of Elements:
3

Number of Sub-Elements:
2

Elem/Sub-Elem Data:
gender:male
name:Jeff Bezos
gender:male
name:Elon Musk
gender:female
name:Jessica Alba
>
```

Using Minidom Module to parse XML

You can also use Minimal Document Object Model (or Mini DOM) module to parse XML documents, however, for security reasons, it is preferred to use the ElementTree module instead.

Using Minidom, you can achieve parsing in three simple steps.

- Import xml.dom.minidom module
- Utilize the function parse (i.e. minidom.parse) to parse the document (minidom.parse ("persons.xml")
- Get the XML Elements using doc.getElementsByTagName("element")

Python Code

```
1   from xml.dom import minidom
2
3   doc = minidom.parse("persons.xml")
4
5   elements = doc.getElementsByTagName("element")
6   for element in elements:
7       name = element.getElementsByTagName("name")[0]
8       gender = element.getElementsByTagName("gender")[0]
9       print("name:%s, gender:%s" %
10          (name.firstChild.data, gender.firstChild.data))
```

Code Output

```
Python 3.7.4 (default, Jul  9 2019, 00:06:43)
[GCC 6.3.0 20170516] on linux


name:Jeff Bezos, gender:male
name:Elon Musk, gender:male
name:Jessica Alba, gender:female
>
```

JSON Parsing in Python

JSON is a language-agnostic data encoding standard. It supports primitive types such as strings and numbers along with nested lists and objects.

Python includes a native JSON package that you can use to both encode and decode data. You can use "import json" to import the entire package and parse JSON data into a python dictionary or list. You can parse the JSON file using the json.load() into python dictionary data structure which is organized in key-value pairs. You can also read and write JSON strings using json.loads() and json.dumps methods respectively.

JSON Document

```
[
  {
    "gender": "male",
    "name": "Jeff Bezos"
  },
  {
    "gender": "male",
    "name": "Elon Musk"
  },
  {
    "gender": "female",
    "name": "Jessica Alba"
  }
]
```

Python Code

```
1  import json
2  with open('persons.json', 'r') as f:
3      my_dict = json.load(f)
4
5  for distro in my_dict:
6      print(distro['gender'])
7      print(distro['name'])
```

Code Output

```
Python 3.7.4 (default, Jul  9 2019, 00:06:43)
[GCC 6.3.0 20170516] on linux
male
Jeff Bezos
male
Elon Musk
female
Jessica Alba
>
```

YAML Parsing in Python

YAML is the most human-friendly data encoding or serialization standard out there. Much like JSON, it is also a language-agnostic data encoding method. You can use the PyYAML library to read and write YAML data.

You can import pyYAML library using "import yaml" and then load YAML file into python dictionary object or data structure using yaml.safe_load() method. You can use yaml.dump() method to write YAML.

YAML Document

```yaml
---
- gender: male
  name: Jeff Bezos
- gender: male
  name: Elon Musk
- gender: female
  name: Jessica Alba
...
```

Python Code

```python
import yaml
with open('persons.yaml', 'r') as f:
    my_dict = yaml.safe_load(f)

for distro in my_dict:
    print(distro['gender'])
    print(distro['name'])
```

Code Output

```
Python 3.7.4 (default, Jul  9 2019, 00:06:43)
[GCC 6.3.0 20170516] on linux
male
Jeff Bezos
male
Elon Musk
female
Jessica Alba
>
```

Further Reading
Python syntax, I/O, conditionals, and functions[23]
Python data structures and loops[24]
Parsing JSON using Python[25]
XML Basics[26]

---

[23] https://bit.ly/339zydy

[24] https://bit.ly/2TGYN3H

[25] https://bit.ly/3cTRMUU

[26] https://bit.ly/2wTrJwg

Chapter Summary

- Controller-based management can fully take advantage of software-driven innovation esp. AI and ML in the areas of provisioning, monitoring, and operations
- The concept of overlays, i.e. virtual topology built on top of a physical network, started with SDN and DC networking. However, with the advent of SD-WAN, the overlays made their way into WAN.
- Data plane (traffic that is not sourced or destined from/to the device, i.e., transit traffic)
- Southbound APIs facilitate efficient control over the network infrastructure and enable the SDN controller to make changes to the device's data plane dynamically
- Northbound APIs are the most critical APIs in the SDN environment since the value of SDN is also tied to the innovative applications it can potentially support and enable. Northbound APIs utilize REST APIs.
- Cisco DNA Center is at the center of Cisco's intent-based networking initiative.
- REST web service API or REST API is a programming interface that adheres to the principles of REST and communicates over HTTP.
- Idempotency is about producing desired results each time an automation is run. It enables convergence and composability
- JSON and YAML can be converted to each other without much effort. JSON is best known for the curly brace syntax
- JSON data types include numbers, strings, and boolean (True or False). JSON filenames typically end in ".json".
- JSON is a language-agnostic data encoding standard. It supports primitive types such as strings and numbers along with nested lists and objects.

www.ingramcontent.com/pod-product-compliance
Lightning Source LLC
Chambersburg PA
CBHW080454220526
45465CB00006B/2272